Contagious Love

Carol!

Thank you so much for supporting me with this book. You were the first author I ever met and only I've interviewed haha.

That made a serious impact ~~and~~ as a 2nd grader because I always felt like there was a book in me since I was little.

I hope you enjoy this book!

♡ Ana

Contagious Love

Break Free from Codependency for Damn Good

By Carla Romo

First edition, 2019

ISBN: 9781689772235
Imprint: Independently published

Cover design by Melanie Blanchard Gong
Interior design by Sadie Fienberg
Author photo by Tessie Tracy

Editor's Note: While the stories in this book are real, some names and identifying information have been changed to protect the confidentiality and privacy of the individuals involved.

This publication is not intended as a substitute for the advice of health care or legal professionals.

Dedication

I dedicate this book to "little" Carla and anyone who is struggling to navigate their way through feeling worthy and enough.

It does get a hell of a lot better.

Acknowledgments

My mom
My two sisters
"Monks"
My fierce clients
Ann D., LCSW
Corrine Casanova
Sadie Fienberg

x

CONTENTS

ENDORSEMENTS

Contagious Love is a powerful narrative of self-love and self-worth that everybody can benefit from reading. It's relatable, inspiring, and the perfect guide on how to break free from codependency in any relationship.
- Melissa Hobley, Global Chief Marketing Officer at OkCupid

When it comes to relationships it's extremely hard to look deep inside and ask yourself what you need to change, but that's exactly what Carla Romo does. She healed herself before committing to healing others as a dating and relationship coach. Anyone who has ever been in any kind of toxic relationship, codependent or not, needs to read this book.
- Kris Perelmutter, Author of Breakup Positive

Carla Romo gives her readers the green light to live fiercely, love themselves fearlessly and embrace their inner badass with Contagious Love.
- Shelby Daniel, Casting Producer for relationship series on FOX, TLC, & Netflix

Carla Romo helps women become badass relationship navigators creating the right push to get them on the path to have successful relationships.
- Gina Ruccione, Podcast Host of A Series of Unfortunate Dates

Contagious Love is the roadmap to thriving relationships!
- Christen Chambers, Fortune 500 Executive

Romo guides her readers by shifting them out of codependency and toward tangible action steps to cultivate healthy, intimate relationships.
 - Bruce D Schneider, Founder, iPEC Coaching and Author of Energy Leadership and Uncovering the Life of your Dreams

INTRODUCTION

I never asked for an abusive father. I never asked for the daddy issues or the absence of self-love that came with it. Still, here I was hyperventilating at age seven because Noah no longer wanted to be my boyfriend. Heartbreaking? Not exactly. I just moved on to a new boyfriend a few days later.

Over and over again, I "picked" a guy, some toxic shit went down, and we broke up. You know, the song, *Thank U Next*, Ariana Grande style except *not* learning after each ex.

I'm a firm believer to keep failing until you succeed, but I got to be real with you, girl. That shit isn't cute when it comes to relationships. Why? It's like banging your head against the wall hoping the headache will stop. Trust me, not even popping four ibuprofen will help your head.

I was holding myself back from living my best life. I was miserable, and I was afraid of healthy relationships. Hey, it made sense to me, ok?

I couldn't figure out how to get the headache to stop no matter how many failed relationships I was in. It was like driving a car with a blindfold on, not a *50 Shades of Grey* blindfold, but a used makeshift one from a construction dude's sweaty red 1990's bandana. I was turning left, thinking I was turning right. I made a U-turn thinking I was heading straight.

I had no fucking clue where I was going, but I thought I had full control over the car until I didn't. After years of dust trails behind me, I had enough. I slammed my Old Navy sandal on the brakes, the anti-lock kicked in, and I threw that blindfold sucker off.

For the first time in 24 years, I knew I had arrived. Not hyperventilating. Not doing the *Thank U Next* song and dance with men. Not trying to make a man love me. Not fixing anyone else. I was exactly where I was supposed to be. It was me, myself and self-love. My journey breaking free from codependency for damn good had begun.

Learning that I was codependent felt like the missing puzzle piece I'd been on a hunt for. It validated my feelings and past relationships. It allowed me to step into ownership for my past and recognize what I could and could not change.

The best part of all of this is that I wasn't living in the circus alone. Although it's difficult to say how many people suffer from codependency traits, they say over 90 percent of Americans have codependent behavior. Well, ok, that's a lot. So, you may or may not be codependent. But the fact that I wasn't unique in this madness made me feel right at home.

Self-love is the foundation of successful relationships. No matter what crazy shit you've been through, it's still possible to have healthy relationships if you take care of yourself first. It's like the airline video demonstrating that you need to put your oxygen mask on first. It's the same in relationships. You can't save others before saving yourself.

I'm not saying that by reading this book you will no longer be codependent and you'll magically have zero relationship issues. I can be the first to tell you that I have had non-codependent relationships and they are not perfect. I'm not asking you to strive for perfection here. All I am asking is that you find the courage to believe in yourself enough to invest in you.

I used to feel shame around being codependent. I thought I was damaged, fucked up, and needed to hold it in. When you hold shit in, let's face it, girl, it only builds within. I could never have imagined writing a book with the name codependent in the title: me, the author of a book on codependency. So, if you're there or not yet, it's ok to feel shame, guilt, confused, etc. I've been there, I've done that, and I've broken free from codependency.

You've freaking made it! You might have opened this damn book to learn something about codependency. You may even be sipping on your matcha wondering, "How the hell do I fix my relationship issues?" Well, I've got you, girl. You want answers, and I've got solutions.

Throughout the book, I share my personal story and impactful client stories revealing what it takes to really love yourself. I've got a damn good formula for breaking free from codependent relationships that I will be sharing with you throughout the book.

In *Contagious Love*, love has no boundaries. It's for the single chick, the married wife, and the woman who is going through heartbreak. I try to keep it as real as possible 'cause that's how I roll. Heads up, I drop an F-bomb here and there. As my mother would say, "You've been cussing like a sailor since age five." True story—my next-door neighbors from Washington state taught me how to cuss up a storm, but that's a whole other book for another time.

But for real, how bad do you want to steer your own damn car? Are you ready to make this change? You can keep going back and forth in your mind. But the more you swing that pendulum, the more you stay stuck. This is your moment; this is your shot. It's time to step into the relationship with yourself.

K, now turn the page.

CHAPTER 1
MAKE A CHANGE

Not every day do you wake up and say, "Ah, I think I'll become a dating and relationship coach." And to be quite honest, the question I get most often is, "How do you become a dating and relationship coach?"

Well, the answer is quite simple. You go through some fucked up codependent relationships repeatedly until you can't take it. You say something's got to change. From there, you do some serious inner work, like that *deep* shit, and learn tools for a healthy relationship. Then, you apply it to your life.

Basically, you transform your life so much that you think other women must be going through similar situations. Eureka, they totally are! That's when I knew all that shitty relationship stuff I went through served a purpose in my life. It helped me grow stronger, independent, and break free of codependency for damn good so that I could help other women gain confidence and purpose in their dating lives, relationships, and breakups.

What Exactly is Codependency?

Let me break this codependency shit down for you real quick. 'Cause what's the point of this book if you don't know the delio behind it, right?

Author Melody Beattie defines codependency in her groundbreaking book, *Codependent No More*, as "one who has let another person's behavior affect him or her, and who is obsessed with controlling that person's behavior." Then we've got Merriam-Webster dictionary over here defining it as a psychological condition or a relationship in which a person is controlled or manipulated by another who is affected with a pathological condition (such as an addiction to alcohol or heroin).

But, here's the catch, according to an article, *The Relationships Between Codependency and Femininity and Masculinity,* in the scholarly journal, Sex Roles, "There are numerous definitions of codependency provided in the literature, but no definition has achieved a consensus of acceptance, and none has been empirically derived."[1] So, long story short, no one could agree on the official definition, but there were a few reviewers who concluded there are core characteristics of codependency with the most common theme being an excessive reliance on other people for approval and identity.

So, you don't have to be in a relationship with an alcoholic to be codependent. Codependency thrives in one-sided, emotionally destructive, or abusive relationships. Let's move on.

My Story

I grew up with domestic violence. My father was abusive. Chaos was my norm. My father left when I was about two years old. But I should use *left* lightly. He'd come back and ring the doorbell, harass the family and threatened to kidnap my sisters and me. It was terrifying as a child, and I suffered from PTSD because of it. You may be gasping, or you may find comfort in knowing you're not the only one with a dysfunctional upbringing.

From the young age of four, I fantasized about marrying a man who would save me. That's why Disney movies are toxic in the best codependent way possible. They feed pre-exposed codependent children with more fantasy. Even in pre-school, I had boyfriends. I loved the idea of someone liking me as it gave me confidence and validation. It felt as if all my problems were diminished. I recall these feelings so well even though I was only four years old.

Please Save Me from My Life

In the first grade, I had one of the first anxiety attacks I can remember. Noah no longer wanted to be my boyfriend. Devastated, I burst into uncontrollable tears on the recess playground. I was so hysterical they had to call my middle sister out of her fourth-grade class to come and comfort me. Some say that's young heartbreak. I say that's giving someone else enough power that you feel like you can't live without them AKA dependent AF.

Fast forward a few grades, and there was Liam. He was a tall Italian boy with some cool dark, fluffy hair. I was a decade old, and I had a magnetic pull to Liam. There was something so attractive about him. All I wanted was for him to like me.

Somehow, he didn't seem to care much about me. When we were "boyfriend" and "girlfriend," he kissed another girl. I dumped him, of course, and then one week later I wanted him back. There was something about fighting for a love that felt comforting and horrible all at once. Eventually, Liam became an addict and ended up dying from a heroin overdose 14 years later.

Cut to middle school. I so badly wanted to fit in. I hung out with the cool and popular kids, yet I felt far from it. I went through boyfriend after boyfriend in middle school. I even broke up and went back out with the same boy six times. I needed to feel needed.

High school brought me Ethan, who I dated for almost two years. That relationship was toxic as hell. I felt stuck and didn't know how to get out. At age 15, I told him for us to continue seeing each other he needed to go to therapy. Well, he didn't go to therapy, and we didn't continue dating.

In college, there was Harper. We became official shortly after knowing one another. However, the first time he asked me to be his girlfriend, I said no. It didn't feel right. About three days later, I went back and said yes. He couldn't speak up for the life of him. I stayed for three and a half years, even though he never shared his thoughts or feelings and was emotionally vacant. It ended shortly after I moved to LA with a plan he would follow. The relationship ended via a phone call where he confessed he no longer was in love with me. The truth later surfaced that he did indeed cheat on me.

Do you get the point? I was in one codependent relationship after another. And if I didn't serve a purpose in changing my boyfriend's fucked up life, then I didn't feel connected. Here's the deal: I was so fucked up that I needed to find someone equally fucked up; otherwise, they wouldn't get how fucked up I was. Well, that's at least what I thought.

The Allure of the Unattainable—Jake

I met Jake when I was 22 at a mutual friend's birthday party. He could start a conversation with anyone and everyone. I found this attractive. He was ten years older than me. Immediately my gut felt off, although he was confident and outgoing. Why would a 32-year-old want to date a 22-year-old? He would bring up his ex-girlfriend all the time. He said they were done, but it just didn't sit right with me. After two months of dating, we mutually broke it off. I'll go into the "mutual" part later. Even though it was over, he kept checking in with me, but I was never interested in a friendship.

About six months later, I started dating Daniel, who had a serious mental illness that he was not handling. He was strong as hell and brilliant. We instantly bonded on our first hiking date. I told him all about my upbringing, and it felt safe because he too had family dysfunction. But I broke things off after two months because he was suicidal.

Two days after my breakup with Daniel, my phone lit up with a text from Jake. It was if he knew somehow that I was lonely and had just ended things with Daniel. From that point on, I went from leaving one codependent relationship to entering my last with Jake. As the months grew, so did the chaos in my relationship with Jake. Over time, he became less interested in me yet more controlling. I worked around his schedule, plans, mood, and happiness. And I was totally game.

He had a way of crafting his arguments from being passive-aggressive to "only wanting the best for me, *but...*" If I had an opinion or thought about something, it would always end up changing to whatever he wanted. If I thought I smelled another woman's perfume on the passenger seat belt the conversation quickly changed and I didn't even notice. He was artistic with his manipulation. It's like he had studied people, knew what made them tick and gently created situations where he'd come out on top.

It fucking worked—until it didn't. Eight months into our relationship, I felt so much shame that I kept it to myself. I judged myself for staying with someone who made negative comments about my friends and family and treated me poorly but always had "the best reason" as to why.

He asked me how many men I slept with so he could make sure I wasn't "a little slut." He told me he couldn't say he loved me because love meant you'd give up the world for another person. He said I wouldn't do that for him, and neither would he do that for me; therefore, we didn't love each other. He called my best friend a slut after sleeping with someone. When I pushed back and got upset, he justified why her actions were slutty. He said he was, "calling it like it is." He talked shit about my sister's boyfriend repeatedly saying that he didn't actually care for my sister, which wasn't true.

Jake would tell me all about his crazy exes and how they never trusted him with their phone. He said to build trust in our relationship; I need never ask to see his phone or look at it. If I held his phone to view driving directions, he would quickly pull it away from my hands.

He was good at playing mind games too. He told me he couldn't come to an important Crossfit competition of mine because he made plans to hang out with his guy friends. Disappointed, I had to accept he wasn't going to be there. Then, right before I went out to compete, he magically appeared looking as if he was doing me a huge favor. Sometimes despite not answering my phone calls or texts throughout the day, he'd show up at my place at 11 pm throwing rocks at my window to wake me up for a surprise visit.

I felt stuck. I began justifying Jake's behavior because I couldn't accept reality. I pushed away my self-worth and self-love somewhere deep within my body. I sat in this space for a few more months. So, I did the only thing I knew. I tried to change him into someone he would never be.

I suggested he go to therapy to deal with his wounded childhood issues. I thought if he went to therapy, he would learn to love himself and then could love me. In my mind, he needed fixing, and I wanted to be the one to fix him.

As I repeatedly tried to fix him, I got nowhere. Doing the same thing over and over again and expecting different results is insanity. He said he would go to therapy and didn't. He said he'd work on saying that he loved me, but he didn't. I was somehow hopeful he'd change into the person I wanted him to be.

His not being able to say he loved me led the relationship to a darker place, but I was relentless. I had to make it work. I wasn't going to give up just yet. As time went on, he became more manipulative and threatening. I didn't see it that way though. I continued to justify his behavior. He'd act out toward me and then apologize. I believed that he'd change as he told me he wanted to and saw where he went wrong.

One night I tried to break up with him. I finally had clarity that he wasn't going to change and felt it was ok to go our separate ways. He countered by saying he would go to therapy. My gut told me to end it while my ego couldn't let him go. I needed a more definitive reason to break up with him. I started searching for an out. And then came the comment that tipped it all.

I was dunking my big spoon into a deep bowl of pho chatting with two girlfriends I met through Jake. They were dating his guy friends.

Disclaimer: Sketchy people surround themselves with sketchy people.

My friend Selena's boyfriend at the time was, well, sketchy with other women. We were discussing her situation, and I commented about Jake saying her boyfriend was sketchy. She turned and looked at me and said, "Yeah, well, what does that say about Jake, then?" And at that moment, I had my answer. She knew something about Jake that I didn't.

That evening I brought up her comment to Jake

when he came over to my apartment. He went from 0-100 real quick. As I tried to calm him, he swatted his arm at me, pushing me away. Mentally, I blacked out. The next thing I knew, he was calmly telling me that we both made mistakes, and I was asking to be hit by getting in his way. That night, I tried to end it with him, but once again, we ended up together on his terms.

The Trip of a Lifetime

Two weeks after our fight, I left for an already planned solo trip to Ireland. Do you know that feeling where you're magnetically drawn to do something? That's what planning this trip was for me.

I had traveled around the world and even studied abroad in Florence, Italy, for a semester, but this was different. For the first time, I was traveling alone and only relying on myself. I was completely out of my comfort zone. It was scary as shit, exciting, and thrilling.

I was putting myself first. It was empowering. When I arrived in Ireland, my goal was to make it to my hotel safe and then figure out my tourist plan of action. After I checked into my hotel, I tried to reach out to Jake, but he wasn't responding. I felt suspicious and checked his Instagram. He had just "liked" a wet t-shirt photo of a woman he worked with at the gym. I felt icky, but there was no way in hell I was going to let his lack of communication disrupt my adventure.

I put my black Steven Madden combat boots on and stepped foot into this historic city. The shops and pubs fronts looked like something out of a movie. As I was peeking around, I passed a tour guide storefront and decided to go in. An older looking woman greeted me with a thick Irish accent and red scarf. She opened her tour guidebook, pointed at a picture of lush green trees, and told me I needed to go to the Wicklow Mountains. I had no clue where that was, but I decided, fuck it, this is the time to be spontaneous and go for it. On a map, she circled where the tour bus would pick me up at 8 am the next morning.

I woke up, hit a Crossfit workout, showered, and made my way to the bus stop with 15 minutes to spare. I'm well known for the Carla Romo dash, AKA running through airports, because I wait until the last minute, but not this time. Plus, I had paid 25 Euro for it. I stood and waited until 30 minutes past the pickup time. I knew something was wrong. Confused, I walked back to the tour guide store.

When I walked in, the same older woman who signed me up for the adventure greeted me. She looked at the time she wrote down and gasped. Turning the same color as her red scarf, she said, "My apologies. I completely wrote down the wrong time. I put 8 am, and your tour was for 7 am."

I was annoyed, jetlagged, and tired. I could feel my eyes tear up but quickly pulled it together. My attitude shifted. I only had two nights in Ireland with one full day left. I wasn't going to let this ruin my day. The woman quickly pulled out a sizeable colorful tourist map highlighting the local bus route. She explained that I could still visit if I took the local bus to the Wicklow Mountains. I wondered if missing that 7 am bus was a sign I wasn't supposed to go. Although, like anything in life, if you're meant to do something, the universe will always get you to where it wants you to be.

I walked from one side of Dublin to the other to get to the bus stop. After 30 minutes, the bus finally came. It was an older run-down bus—not like the nice ones you see in a big city. It made its way winding down country roads with stops at random pubs in bumfuck-nowhere. I had zero clue where I was going but was soaking in the utterly breathtaking and beautiful surroundings.

Destination Inner Peace

Surrounded by luscious green and overcome with peace, I got off the bus. I had never felt so connected to nature in my life. As I walked about the forest, I spoke my thoughts aloud. And no, there was no one around to witness a 24-year-old American woman talking to herself in the middle of nowhere Ireland.

I got lost in my thoughts and continued walking along a winding path. Unexpectedly, a sheet of comfort came over my body, and I saw two different paths in front of me:

1. Continue living a life of self-sabotage.
2. Step into self-love and form an authentic, loving relationship with myself.

I felt deep within that I was too valuable and worthy to continue down this path. Something told me that no matter what was going to happen, I would be ok and I was already ok. This was the first spiritual moment

I acknowledged. Something miraculous came over me that would change my entire life. It was as if I was given a secret that was always meant to be mine. The answer on what to do was within me the entire time. For the first time, I had the strength and courage to listen.

This trip shifted something far greater than I could have anticipated. It was time to leave the mushroom pies, tea, and boxty of Dublin. I hopped on the plane to LAX where Jake was waiting to pick me up in a long ass line of cars. He greeted me with a kiss, and in my heart, I knew our relationship was over. I no longer needed to be with him. It was fucking done.

The next day, I invited our mutual friend Katy over to my apartment for dinner. Toward the end of dinner, I point-blank asked her if Jake had cheated on me. Those words sat at the tip of my tongue, and I finally had the courage to listen. She tilted her head down and said there were rumors he had been sleeping with the front desk girl at his Crossfit gym.

Suddenly, everything was so clear. Maybe the answers were always in front of me, but this time, I was ready to receive them. I headed over to Jake's apartment and tried to break up with him. He told me that I was not acting "normal" or "sane." He said I needed to reconsider, go home, and get some rest. I left his apartment feeling more confused than ever.

Was I insane? Was I not acting normal?

The next morning, I called my therapist to tell her about the situation. She said, "I'm not saying he is abusive, but what he is saying to you is considered abusive behavior." It clicked. It finally fucking clicked. I wasn't crazy. I never was crazy. I was dating someone abusive.

I grabbed my keys and drove over to his apartment, kept it brief, broke up with him, and ran out of his apartment. He chased me down the steps yelling at me to get back inside. I drove off. After the breakup, like typical abusers, he reached out several times from different phone numbers, and email addresses. He even showed up on my doorstep with an abundance of gifts.

The breakup with Jake was monumental. It gave me a chance to stare codependency in the face and cultivate a new awareness. It was as if all the puzzle pieces to my dysfunctional relationships came together. I no longer had to carry out this pattern.

How do you know if you're codependent?

Maybe you've sat in your therapist's office and heard the words, "That's codependency." Maybe you thought, "What the fuck is that?" Or maybe you find yourself trying to fix your partner's addiction or just obsessing over the relationship.

Think of codependency as depending on someone else's life for your own happiness and well-being. It's a cycle that goes on and on. But I'm not going to leave you hanging, girlfriend. Otherwise, why the hell would I be writing this book? It's time to get involved.

The Codependency Test

Directions: Place a checkmark next to each statement you can relate to in either your current or past relationships:

☐ Trouble saying no
☐ Not compromising with your partner
☐ Obsessing over your relationship situation or the person you're dating
☐ Not breaking up with your partner even when you know it's the right choice
☐ Feeling you know what's best for your partner
☐ Not putting your needs first
☐ Believing your partner will change when there is little action
☐ Wanting to please your partner
☐ Putting full blame on your partner
☐ Feeling trapped in a relationship
☐ Your mood or feelings depend upon your partner
☐ Reacting to when disagreeing
☐ Justifying or denying someone else's behavior or addiction
☐ Avoiding conflict with your partner
☐ Not feeling good enough. Feeling alone or not worthy (any or all)
☐ Worried your partner won't love you
☐ Afraid your partner will leave
☐ Not practicing self-care (getting six to eight hours of sleep, eating three meals, routine exercise)
☐ Making excuses or lies to protect your partner
☐ Bringing up past problems or arguments
☐ Feeling uncomfortable when there is no chaos

Even if you only checked one box, you may have

codependency characteristics or traits. Time to carry on now!

What Codependency Looks Like

Meg had been in a relationship with Rick who let's just say spent more weekends with his Jack Daniels than he did with Meg. He couldn't hold a steady job, but there was always a good reason. He couldn't always pay his rent on time, but that's because his checks didn't line up. He'd get texts from random girls Meg didn't know, but they were just friends from work.

Meg saw the potential in Rick, like big time. He was aware that he needed to make certain changes in his life, but when it came to actions, his words spoke louder. Over time, Meg felt the need to pick up the neglected pieces Rick left behind. Eventually, Meg did so much for Rick that she thought she knew what was best for him. This enabled his behavior, and as a result, Rick had no serious consequences of not taking care of himself.

During this time, Meg lost a sense of her own self because she spent so much time making sure Rick was happy and doing what he was supposed to. When Meg began working with me, she had pushed aside so many of her own needs that putting herself first felt selfish. It wasn't until she was aware that she was in a codependent relationship that she could start making changes to better the relationship with herself, so her relationship with Rick could grow.

McKenzie basically dated the same guy twice but with a different face. She hired me after she realized she no longer wanted to fall into the trap again. Who was the same guy? Let's just start by saying he didn't have his shit together. She went after guys who were deep talkers, spontaneous, and charismatic. There were red flags, but she was able to justify them. One of McKenzie's guys fell into mismanaging his finances while the other watched excessive porn. McKenzie chose to look the other way because she felt that she could see beyond their imperfections.

Eventually, McKenzie found out they both cheated on her. Both boyfriends made a promise not to do it ever again and vowed to make it up to her. Even though she knew it wasn't right, she felt trapped and stayed. In return, she felt shame and guilt for continuing to date men, who treated her poorly.

By the end of her second relationship, she doubted she would date again. McKenzie worked with me to build trust and confidence in herself so she would never make the same mistake again.

Two Ways to Recognize Codependency

Many of us don't realize when we are in a codependent relationship, even if we do recognize the symptoms. We don't want to let the relationship go. There are two things that can help you recognize codependency:

1. Listen to your gut.
2. Take responsibility for making changes in your life.

Listen to Your Gut

That shit does not lie. If something feels totally off in your relationship, well, it probably is. Let's just be honest here; you picked up this book to learn more about codependency. Why? Because it's hard to figure out if your relationship is codependent. It ain't easy. It isn't like you can take your temperature and boom—if it's over 99.1° F, you're codependent.

It can feel so freaking confusing when you're "in it." The chaos can feel like love because when there is no chaos, there is no love. Recall a time when you were in chaos and thought that might be your normal. Chances are at some point; you had your wait a minute moment and asked, "What the hell have I gotten myself into?" It's the sweet spot of "wait a minute" that you need to pay attention to. As I coach my clients, wait a minute moments come out in different ways and it's often how we find our rock bottom and decide to do something about it. That intuitive feeling in your gut helps with this. Others find it getting quiet or gathering enough evidence to say enough is enough.

As the wait a minute moment happens, you often recognize you can't continue like this and find your rock bottom. When I was dating Daniel, who had become suicidal, I knew this was something much greater than I could handle. I knew that if I continued to date him, I would want to watch over his every move and try to save him from his own life choices. That was my rock bottom. There was nothing I could do to save him. My gut knew it was time to end the relationship. I didn't want to, but I knew I needed to put myself first. I knew it would cause more mental harm for me to stay in the relationship than to leave. My gut was telling me to do what I needed to do to help myself.

When you hit your rock bottom, it's possible not to stay stuck there. You can swim through your rock bottom. Before, when it was time to end a relationship, I thought I would be stuck at the bottom gasping for air with an anchor tied around my ankle. I discovered the anchor only existed in my mind. It's fear, lack of self-worth, and self-love that kept me feeling like I'd be at the bottom forever. It doesn't have to be this way.

The reality is your thoughts and fears always evolve. Life always gives you opportunities to swim through the pain and struggle. It's your mind that keeps you thinking there is no way out.

Take Responsibility to Make Changes in Your Life

Welcome, girlfriend! You're in confident warrior territory. At some point, you've got to open those badass eyes of yours and say, "Alright girl, let's make some changes so I can feel damn good about myself." Maybe you are saying, "I can't continue dealing with this shit anymore. I can't go on this way." At some point, you've got to say, "I am taking ownership of what I can do, and that's making some changes."

I'm not saying bypass the emotional stage of grief, a breakup, or feelings toward your current partner. What I am saying is you *do* have control over your actions.

Are you ready? Are you pumped to make that change in your current relationship or with the next person you date? There's no more time for B.S. It's time to put yourself first.

How do you take your newfound awareness of being codependent and make a change that lasts? Glad you asked. You need to be ready to do it. Let me put it this way: change is the only way out.

The Only Way Out

It can be scary as hell to say, "OK, I am ready to change." Taking action to make a change can be terrifying. Most people like to stay in their comfort zone. Most people don't take the time to learn to date in a new way. But you're not like most people, girl! You're someone that recognizes something needs to change. You know deep within that it's time. If you don't, then you will continue to keep following the same cycle that's on that damn washing machine. And girl, you're not a washing machine.

It's time to take full responsibility for your actions and step into the badass woman you are. Imagine you're standing at the top of the mountain with all your exes, relationships, past or current relationship patterns, and problems behind you. You're terrified to step off the mountain because you have no idea what to expect. Yes, it's intimidating, but you're never going to be pushed off the mountain.

This entire time you've been told that if you step off, you'll meet the ground pretty quickly. But what you don't realize is there is a net below you. You're not even going to feel that roller coaster feeling in your stomach. #Barf. Real change doesn't work by catapulting yourself off the mountain. It works by taking the first step down to the net that's always been one foot below you.

Before taking that first step, determine if you are ready to break up or make up. How will you know? In Chapter 2, you'll find out what you need to do to figure out what the hell you want, girlfriend. As Taylor Swift would say, "Are you ready for it?"

 Damn Good Affirmation: #IAmStrengthAndCourage

 Write an empowering statement where you found the strength to take your first step into growth.

Notes:

1. G.E. Dear and C.M. Roberts, The Relationships Between Codependency and Femininity and Masculinity, *Sex Roles*, 46: March 2002, 159.

SHOULD I MAKE UP OR BREAK UP?

It's easy to blame your current partner or ex for the shit they put you through. Or maybe your parents are to blame because of their fucked-up relationship you witnessed as a child. Now that you know you're not crazy, just codependent, you can't help but realize every little thing your current partner, ex, or date has done to make you feel crazy. This includes telling little lies, using you, manipulating you, embarrassing you, and making you feel like a crazy person.

Disclaimer: We're all a little crazy, but those people have occupied enough free rent in your mind. It's time to kick the obsession out!

You might be asking, "How did I fall into this trap?" Once you are aware and understand how it happened, it now becomes a choice. It's time you put the power back into those powerful, strong, resilient, worthy hands of yours. Are you ready for it?

From Victor to Survivor - Becoming Damn Good at Being a Badass

Ready to move from victim to survivor? By making

this move, you no longer have to endure being pushed around, thinking there isn't a way out. Being stuck with the burden of making it work out is no longer a reality. Chances are you were conned by someone who has an addiction or some sort of mental illness. It's important to recognize that the other person has a disease if it's addiction or they're mentally ill. This doesn't excuse their behavior toward you, but with this understanding, it can help you lead with compassion.

I truly believe in the saying, opposites attract. As a codependent, you will naturally want to feel loved and validated, so you may go for someone who feels extremely validated and loved. You know, like a narcissist. Narcissists are like vacuums to codependents. They'll suck up all the love and attention you give them and give nothing back in return. It's sorta like Meryl Streep's character in *The Devil Wears Prada*. She legit has no problem letting her assistant bend over backward for her needs. But the catch is, the assistant is a people pleaser, afraid to say no, and looking for worth and validation in this boss versus assistant relationship.

I'll never forget sitting in my therapist's office and first realizing I was a victim of domestic violence as a child. She responded, "You're no longer a victim; you're a survivor." It's that goosebump moment that pulsed badass courage and strength through my body.

You're entering what I like to call the beginning of the badass phase—going from Victim to Survivor. You recognize there is a time and place to be a victim and a survivor. Once you're hit with that awareness or ah-ha, you have choices. You're no longer stuck. It's time to get out of the victim mode and take ownership like a mother fuckin' boss lady.

You Call the Shots

There is nothing more empowering than recognizing it's time to take ownership. No one is telling you what to do or how to do it. It's your responsibility. This is where you get to own your value, realizing you are worthy and enough. Even just sitting doing nothing, you're worthy and enough.

It's ok to feel batshit terrified. It means that change is a-brewing. This is where the change happens. For life to continue propelling you forward, change is necessary. You're only guaranteed one thing in life, and that is nothing will ever be the same.

No matter how much you try to manipulate change by staying stagnant or ignoring awareness, change is 100 percent guaranteed. You get to decide whether to take part in the change or not engage. Ultimately, the choice is yours. Doing nothing is also a choice because you're actively choosing not to act.

Awareness is the ah-ha moment that hits you like a motherfucker.

You realize you won't put up with the way things have been going anymore. You decide that you've had enough. You've hit your rock bottom or as I like to say, "You're just swimming through it." You know it's time for things to shift and change to occur. Change can look like

27

working on yourself, breaking up with your partner, or dating differently. You get to decide.

Sophia's Story

Sophia is the type of badass women who drives a BMW, has an MBA, and is an executive at a media company. She has her shit together, and her life is lined up perfectly, except for her seven-year on and off relationship with Ryan.

The relationship was never defined. She wanted the relationship, but he insisted that he wasn't looking for what she wanted. So, they played a game of ping-pong going back and forth between dating others and getting back together. She felt connected to him and so badly wanted him to change his mind, so she stuck around.

She knew in her gut that this relationship wasn't right. He wanted to go on dates but did not want to commit. He didn't want kids, and she did. When she wanted to back off from the relationship, he didn't respect her space.

Sophia spent her 30's in this relationship. It felt wrong but comfortable. She felt she could be herself, felt butterflies when they were together, and felt a true connection. Despite this, she never considered him as her boyfriend. He didn't want that. He wanted to reap the benefits of sex and spending time together without commitment. And she let him.

It wasn't until we dug deeper that she realized she had allowed him to call the shots. As a result, she would stay quiet to avoid conflict and brush off her feelings. Naturally, she liked the attention he gave her.

Sophia's ah-ha moment came when she recognized she had a choice.

She could continue this relationship even though it was not what she wanted, or she could follow-through on her personal love goals. With her ah-ha, she took her awareness and put it into action. She broke things off with Ryan in an amicable way. This wasn't easy for her. She went back and forth about doing so for a couple of sessions. Ultimately, she chose to act on her new awareness, knowing it would lead her to what she really wanted. Putting herself first in this relationship after seven years of putting herself second gave her value and worth.

Putting Yourself First

Putting yourself first, as Sophia did, is a great start. You no longer feel trapped once you have your ah-ha.

You can finally say peace out to black and white thinking. Maybe it's breaking up with your current partner, ending the occasional back and forth small talk for good with your ex, or being the change in your current relationship. You have total control over how you want to spend your life. You get to choose whether you stay or go.

Cutting off communication with an ex or ending a current relationship can be difficult, especially if you've tried so hard to make it work. You may feel like you're failing or you can't get any relationship right. You might feel shame about what people will think. You may not acknowledge the relationship is over.

Focusing on yourself and your needs first will help drive the action of your ah-ha. If you're making a blind decision by acting out on your fear or feelings, then you're going to keep going in circles. Most likely, this will leave you wondering if it's the right choice for you, and if you've made a mistake.

Choices are about showing up for yourself. That shit ain't easy. Insert Bambi learning to walk for the first time. Move forward by placing one foot in front of the other. You no longer have to be a prisoner of your own thoughts.

Charlie's Ah-ha

Ah-ha's can feel a bit intimidating. This is an opportunity to think differently.

Disclaimer: Often, what we resist the most in life is our key to inner self-freedom and happiness.

If you choose to stay in your current relationship, then work on what *you* are responsible for. Charlie had been dating Max for over a year, and there clearly was a lack of communication. Things were getting rocky. They were living together and talked about living separately while still dating. Charlie's ah-ha was she was completely neglecting her life.

She was no longer participating in hobbies and pushed off making girlfriends or hanging out with friends. As she wanted to stay in her relationship with Max, she knew the only thing she could change was her attitude and behavior. The lack of balance in the relationship put a lot of strain and pressure on her. She felt that if they broke up, she'd have nothing.

Over time, Charlie recognized she had a choice in and power over her part of the relationship. She didn't need to make decisions based on the fear she'd have nothing if they broke up. She recognized it was time to work on the relationship and not live in fear of breaking up.

Charlie didn't allow her ah-ha to cripple her. Instead, it empowered her to act. She saw that she could choose reality over fear. Was this easy for her? No. It took a couple of trial and errors until she felt confident. But that's how confidence works. It's taking Bambi steps, looking back, and recognizing you are worthy.

All in or All Out

An ah-ha happens when we allow ourselves to accept what is happening fully. That's when we see we have choices. I used to feel afraid to be alone. Immediately after one relationship ended, I'd be dating someone new. It wasn't until I recognized this behavior that I chose to spend six months without any dating, sex, kissing, etc. It was hard. I'm not even going to lie.

Let's face it. I knew my purpose in doing so was more powerful than an orgasm with some dude during sex. Instead, I worked on building a relationship with myself. This was my choice as I didn't want to fall into the same behavior patterns again and again. Being so quick to date wasn't going to get me where I wanted to be.

We're all different. After a breakup, maybe you need to find another boyfriend ASAP, or perhaps you feel that you never want to date again. It's easy to get stuck in this cycle. Maybe you've had an ah-ha, but don't feel comfortable with making a change yet.

Ultimately, it comes down to the same thing. You're thinking too black and white. You see your option as you need someone, like pronto, or you feel you won't ever find love again. That's black and white thinking. You may even recognize you're making excuses too. Acknowledge it and move on.

Being On Your Own No Matter What You Decide

Changing how you show up in relationships can feel like walking into a cheesy-ass Halloween haunted house. You know what you're getting yourself into yet you're afraid of what might pop out at you. It's scary. It's intriguing.

You will find what you thought would scare you isn't scary at all. The people are wearing costumes and are actors. It's your mind that is playing tricks on you. What once frightened you was just something you made up in your mind. You hit your ah-ha and are now aware that you have a choice.

You can still be "on your own" whether you're single or in a relationship. It can feel more comfortable to stay in a bad relationship than it does to be single. Sometimes it's easier to be in a relationship and just complain about it.

It's sitting in that *in-between* hot spot of, "I know I need to change my behavior in my current relationship, or I know this relationship isn't right, but maybe I'm not ready to end things." This is an ah-ha moment. That thought alone is nudging you in the right direction. This will save your ass more times than not. You're no longer wandering around wondering what you're doing wrong. Sure, maybe you question yourself, but you have enough ah-ha to recognize you have choices.

It All Starts with You

It doesn't matter what spectrum of the love line you're on (from breakups to relationships). What matters is that you recognize you're the only person who can truly make a difference. It can be hard to leave finger-pointing and blaming behind, but once you stop finding excuses or justifications for another person's actions and behaviors, you'll stop blaming someone else for yours.

The journey is inside. Outside validation and relationships no longer fulfill you. Are you ready? Some people live their entire lives and don't tap into their journey. It's time for yours to begin.

Whether you decide to attempt to save the relationship, break up, or start a new relationship, you need to lead with your ah-ha first. Trying to change the other person to fit what you want isn't fair to you or them. The key to success in relationships begins with working on yourself first, not changing the other person.

Only you have the power to change yourself.

This change doesn't come overnight. There are a lot of factors to putting on your best heels and walking change into action. Eventually, you will get to a place where you can recognize your ah-ha and navigate life through it.

I'm never going to push you to start dating again, break up with your partner, or stay in a relationship. That's your choice. There is no right or wrong choice. It's just a choice.

Get out of your damn way and fill yourself with respect and self-love. Not sure of the value of self-love? Keep reading, girlfriend! You are about to discover why loving yourself should always come first.

 Damn Good Affirmation: #IAmPuttingMeFirst

 Write about a time you've experienced your own ah-ha moment.

LOVE YA DAMN SELF

Codependency is contagious love. No matter what you do, no matter how much you talk about it, no matter how much you think about it, you can't get rid of it. If you don't deal with it, it'll leave you wondering why you keep ending up with the same type of dysfunctional partner or situation. It's powerful. It's crippling. It's damaging. Codependency is the silent thief robbing you from truly living the love you deserve. What happens if you don't find the self-love and self-worth you deserve? You'll repeat the contagious love pattern over and over again.

Respect Yourself

Get ready to respect yourself. It's time. Be courageous and step into a space of loving yourself. Respect can connect you to self-love. Self-respect equals self-love. It's time to treat yourself with kindness. Show up for yourself. You're valuable and deserve to be treated with love. You are worth it.

For me, a good way to gauge if I'm respecting or loving myself is to think of it like this: if you saw how someone else was being treated in a relationship the way you're being treated in your relationship, would you be ok with that?

Rina kept going out with Jim, who always stood her up. We're not talking once or twice but like five times. They would make plans to meet, and he wouldn't be there. There was always a great excuse, but it felt off to Rina. She liked his attention and found him fascinating, so she continued in the relationship. By doing so, Rina wasn't respecting herself, which allowed him to treat her disrespectfully.

Rina wasn't at fault for this dude's actions. However, she needed to take responsibility for allowing the situation to continue. Eventually, she called it quits. She was embarrassed that she continued to pursue a guy who showed no interest in her. On a positive note, this helped her recognize she wasn't honoring herself, which allowed Jim to treat her that way.

I thought I respected myself. After all, I was awarded "Most Respectful" second grader in my class. Unfortunately, this didn't include internal respect. If you told me years ago, "Girl, choosing shitty partners who can't show up for you is lack of self-respect," I would have written you off as delusional. But, let's face it; I was the delusional one. I gave so much to my partners to earn their love and respect that I forgot about my own. I put myself on the back burner because I wanted to make sure my partner was happy. I needed them to be ok, so I was ok.

That's not sane thinking. No other person can make you feel ok. As a result, I neglected a huge part of myself. I was waiting for someone else to make my life happy and complete. Look in the mirror and respect your damn self by putting yourself first.

Sometimes it's hard to know where to start when it

comes to self-respect. Self-respect has your back. When you begin to respect yourself, it becomes a building block to respecting your partner. Think of it like treating your partner the way you want to be treated. When you do this and respect yourself, you can show up for someone in a relationship.

In doing so, you build your worth and value. You're no longer a last-minute thought or girl stuck in yet another terrible relationship. You're allowing your inner badass to be damn good at stepping into reality and walk away from a negative narrative.

It's Time to Choose

When you begin doubting yourself, with all due respect, you're mindfucking yourself. You get to choose how you show up in your own life. Here are some tips on how to get some damn self-respect:

1. Recognize your worth.
2. Stop using the past to predict your future.
3. Practice being courageous.
4. Think kind thoughts about yourself.
5. Quit second-guessing your gut.
6. Get back up, even when it feels hard.

What Kind of Backpack Are You Carrying?

Consider your lack of self-respect like a backpack you've been carrying around all these years. It's pretty on the outside, but messy as fuck on the inside. Carrying around all this negative talk is bound to make your back hurt. It's time to acknowledge the aches and pains.

If you are hesitant to open the backpack, keep in mind that you already know what's inside. That's because you've let negative self-talk and messy as fuck become part of you. Recognize that everything you believed to be true no longer gets to hold power over you. If this seems overwhelming, remember you don't have to dump the entire contents out if you don't want to. Sometimes a peek inside is enough to kickstart change from negative to self-respect thinking.

You can choose how you want to rearrange the placement of these items in your life. You can let these things be the driver of your life, or you can take the wheel. If you want to right-size this self-talk, say fuck fear. Ultimately, it's your choice. It's ok to want to hold on to certain thoughts, but it's also ok to let them go. Keep in mind that you're winning by respecting yourself. Ya ain't so bad after all, girlfriend!

Loving Yourself

Self-love truly is the foundation of any relationship you will ever have. It's the mirror to your actions and the fuel to your relationships.

You're onto something sexy when you have self-love. Self-love takes work and practice, and it's not something you'll graduate from. Us codependents have layers of learned behavior that deters us from self-love. I'm not saying it's impossible to have self-love. In fact, it's essential you go after it.

Self-Love is the Water of Life

Think of self-love like a badass flower. It's not afraid to bloom into all sorts of colors, but first, you've got to water it. As the seed, you're planted in the ground. The amount of water you receive affects your roots. Consider your roots to be your relationships, financial situation, career, and spirituality.

Surface level shit sprouts up. This is what most people think needs to be fixed in their life. This includes arguments with your partner who doesn't seem to think he has a drinking problem. Or only being attracted to men who don't quite have their shit together, and going on a second date knowing it's not right. Or continuing to reach out to your ex even when you know it "should" be over.

When that happens, you are not watering your roots with self-love. Surface level sprouts are deeper issues in disguise and a good indicator of what you need to focus on.

If you continue to water your badass flower with lack of self-worth, self-respect, and self-love then expect dysfunctional relationships, dates, and breakups to sprout.

Let's just say I struggled with figuring out how to water my damn seed. I thought I loved myself because of how I appeared externally. I was really bomb at my first career in TV. I hustled my ass off, had my first TV producer title at age 23, and was first in the office and last to leave. I freelanced and never had to look too hard for my next gig.

In a sense, I was addicted to being hired by multiple big network shows. I filled my lack of self-worth with titles and pay bumps. I felt high until I burnt out and the cycle continued. All this external stuff gave me a false sense of validation and worth. It never came from within. I continually had to prove myself. And at times, it cost me my mental health. I was relying on a job and title to fill a hole that could never be filled because they were superficial accolades.

This transferred into my relationships. I would seek a new relationship because I wanted to feel loved. I went from TV show to TV show and from relationship to relationship. Doing so, I found confusing pseudo-love, purpose, importance, and validation. I earned it, but it could easily be taken away by my boyfriend or boss. It was a forever losing mind game I chose to play.

I'd hit this dull, grey, lame as fuck plateau every time. When my relationship grew chaotic, and that TV show didn't hold the same level of excitement, it became just another tiring job. I was back to square one—lonely, unloved, and unlovable.

How to Practice Self-Love

I knew I couldn't do this anymore. At the time, I didn't realize I needed to love myself first. I was living for my intimate relationships with boyfriends and never fully living for me. When I saw what I was doing, I knew I could no longer go on this way. It was time for self-love. I changed my idea of love and then practiced it.

My self-love approach was simple yet effective and powerful. As I started taking care of day to day things, I incorporated the following three-step process.

Love Ya Damn Self: Three-Step Process

1. Ask yourself, "What have I been putting off?"
2. Ask yourself, "What do I want in a partner?"
3. Ask yourself, "What do I want for myself?"

Step 1: What have I been putting off? I began asking myself, "What have I been putting off?" For me, it was time with myself and learning to get to know who I was. I chose to take time off from dating. I had gone from one codependent relationship to another. Relationships gave me that quick fix validation but did shit for what I truly wanted. When I no longer needed to rely on a guy for my self-worth, I gained confidence.

For some, their confidence comes from taking charge of their diet, exercise, travel, or hobbies. These activities play a big part in learning to connect with yourself. When you become so focused on someone else, you forget about yourself. It's time to love ya damn self!

Step 2: What do I want in a partner? I had no fucking clue what I wanted in a partner. So, I started by figuring out my values. I wrote them down on a sticky note and placed them on my bathroom mirror. By doing so, I reminded myself of what was important and what wasn't when finding a partner. I gained respect for myself. I started to understand red flags and why I needed to listen to my damn gut. And then I practiced what I learned about myself. I remembered my self-value on dates, in relationships, and even a breakup. The one thing that remained the same, no matter what was me.

41

Step 3: What do I want for myself? It didn't matter if I went on a bad date or got dumped after living with someone for six months. I found happiness within myself regardless of the good or bad in the situation. My dating mantra was, "Does he fit into my life?" I did not ask if I fit into his life. I no longer needed a man to make me feel valued and loved. I wanted a man who would accept me just as I am. Why? Because I was finally able to accept myself. I realized I wasn't as fucked up after all. Therefore, I shouldn't go after "fucked up" guys.

The biggest shock was that I had enough faith in myself that I could be alone and happy. I knew I needed to feel secure and trust my partner, but I no longer felt this need to have to make it work if the relationship wasn't right. Why? Because I knew I would be ok whether they wanted me or not. Would I be upset if they didn't like me? Yes, I'm not a sociopath, and I do have feelings. But it wasn't about the other person. It was about what I wanted. And for the first time, I began to love the only person I could 100 percent count on, and that was me.

Love Ya Damn Self

The love you give someone reflects the love you have inside yourself. You can't love someone else if you don't love yourself. As fashion icon Diane Von Furstenberg says, "The most important relationship in your life is the relationship you have with yourself. Because no matter what happens, you will always be with yourself."

Lindsey was struggling to find herself. She didn't know what she wanted in a relationship, career, or even her life. As a result, she neglected doing things that connected her to herself. She loved painting and drawing except she hadn't done them in a long time. She told me that painting and drawing used to bring her purpose. Others recognized her for her work. Over time, she felt the burden of a relationship creep in and pushed out the things in life that brought her inner belonging. I suggested she start painting again. She went to the store, bought a canvas, some oils and began to paint.

At our next session, I asked her how it was going. She was finally allowing herself to reconnect with something she felt she had lost. For Lindsey, it wasn't the actual painting that brought her this. It was the act of doing something for herself that was purely for her own enjoyment. This brought Lindsey a deep sense of connection and love for herself.

Lack of Self-love is Self-sabotage

When you begin to form a relationship with yourself, it's like dating someone new. It's awkward. You may feel fucking nervous and want to back out. Yet, there's something exciting and intriguing about being in this place. Maybe you feel a newfound sense of freedom or self-acceptance. Or maybe you're second-guessing yourself and using logic to back out of connecting with self-love.

To put it plain and simple, the lack of self-love is self-sabotage. Sometimes it feels more comfortable to sit in this space because it is familiar. In contrast, making changes toward self-love is unfamiliar. A good check-in to ensure you're not self-sabotaging is to ask yourself, "How am I not loving myself today?"

Observe your feelings and think about what fears you might be buying into. Maybe you're taking action to stop loving yourself by creating arguments with your partner to push them away. Maybe thoughts or feelings of intimacy feel like too much. Or maybe you're keeping quiet and avoiding conflict by not speaking up for yourself when your partner or date does something you're not comfortable with. Being a doormat allows people to come and go as they please while wiping their dirty feet on you.

When I was hosting a workshop for about 50 women, I asked if anyone ever tries to tiptoe around conflict. There was a woman in the second row with a thin frame and hipster glasses who slowly raised her hand. I asked her to give an example. She shared that when her husband makes comments about her terrible driving, she stays quiet. She feels she can't speak up, or he will get angrier. So, she holds in her feelings, and her resentment toward him grows. I asked what stops her from communicating with her partner. Growing up, her parents brushed everything under the rug and wouldn't discuss their feelings.

Self-sabotage is something we all do. You're human. You have fears. You feel uncomfortable with the idea of loving yourself, and as a result, you feel resistance. I challenge you to sit in the discomfort. Being uncomfortable with your feelings never killed anyone. Instead of spending so much time in the negative, look at the positive. Ask yourself, "What is the best thing that could happen if I allowed space to love myself?"

Ava had thoughts of loving herself and needing more

but felt she couldn't live up to it. It was scary for her. For 35 years, negative thinking was her reality, and as a result, she didn't love herself. While in session, I asked, "What would it mean to love yourself?" She simply said, "Fully accepting myself." All these years, she felt she needed to live up to her mother's standards of "supposed to have a man by her side." She didn't consider spending time with herself. Ava felt like she needed a man by her side. Even though she had broken up with her ex, she found a way to follow-up with him. In the back of her mind, she wanted him to see how valuable she was. I finally said to Ava, "What would it mean to provide yourself the care and love that Isaac once gave you?" She responded, "I'm afraid to truly love myself."

I told her to lean into it. Self-love was not something that happened overnight. It's kind of like climbing a mountain. Consider the mountain top to be self-love. Old ways of thinking and not loving yourself are at the bottom of the mountain. If you've ever thought about the possibility of loving yourself, then you've already taken steps up the mountain. No one ever climbed Mount Everest in a day, so I wouldn't expect anyone to find self-love that way either.

Self-love is a process that ebbs and flows. Sometimes you feel like you're killing the self-love game while other days you wonder if you'll ever get there. There is no right or wrong way to do it, but some methods are more effective than others.

Barriers That Get in the Way

The only thing getting in your way of self-love is your

own damn self. Yep. You are the only person responsible for filling yourself with love for your badass self. Sure, you may have come from domestic violence, like me, which triggered codependency or maybe you dated an addict, and that was your trigger. At some point, you must take owner- ship of your actions and step into growth. To get shit done, follow this plan.

Get Shit Done Action Plan

1. Acknowledge inner blocks—why hello demons!
2. Realize it's a work in progress—there ain't no quick fix, girl!
3. Take manageable action steps—you don't need to run the NYC Marathon today!

1. Why hello demons! Start by acknowledging those inner blocks that feel good in your mind but butcher any hope or love in real life. Ask yourself:

- What are you afraid of?
- What is the worst that could happen?
- What stops you from taking action and showing up for yourself?

2. There ain't no quick fix, girl! This is a work in progress. Little by little, start thinking about how you want to move past those blocks. Ask yourself:

- What do you need to do to prepare to make a change?
- How will you know when you are ready to take action?
- If you push fear aside, what would be your first action step?

3. You don't need to run the NYC marathon today! Take manageable action steps. Real inner love evolves when you are willing to be consistent and get back up when you stumble. Take one of the following action steps:

- Create a new affirmation.
- Set a small goal in the morning and accomplish it before you go to bed.
- Say "I love you" to yourself.

Joan was afraid of being alone and not having a man in her life. Instead, she kept guys around who were toxic because it validated her worth. The idea of being alone was more fearful than the reality of her toxic relationships.

Acknowledge your inner blocks. Once you discover what's been stopping you and holding you back, then you can begin to make big girl moves successfully. Too many times, we want a quick fix solution. We slap a band-aid right over our problem for temporary relief. Soon, the wound begins to bleed through the bandage and into our life. If not handled properly, that gash will only get deeper and deeper.

For Joan, she continued to replace her fear with men who ultimately got her nowhere. She went for one quick fix after another. This also prevented her from fully grieving the end of a relationship because she was not allowing space to grow.

Without an action plan, you're fucked. There I said it. It's the blind leading the blind. Once you take a step back and allow yourself to see what has been slowing you down from accomplishing self-love, you can create a plan on how to move forward. It comes down to how much you truly want to grow in this space.

And once you've made a commitment to yourself, then you're already past the hardest obstacle. To hold yourself accountable, check in with a friend.

Self-love is a mental game. It's up to you to carry it out. It's up to you to fill yourself. But it's nothing you can't do! Ready, set, self-love on, lady! You are about to meet someone who will help you find the way to self-love—your confident warrior.

 Damn Good Affirmation: #IAmWorthy

 List three ways you will practice self-love.

BE THE CONFIDENT WARRIOR

How do you get the courage to move forward and take on living a full life that includes healthy relationships with not only yourself but others? You do this by tapping into your confident warrior—this unstoppable force within you. Maybe you haven't met her yet. Trust me; she's there. She was there when I needed her, and she will be there for you too.

The confident warrior has been through some shit. She's had her hands dirty, but she's not about to back the fuck down. Deep in your soul, the confident warrior gives you this feeling that nobody can touch you. This confidence has been wanting to be unleashed for years. You have the strength, courage, and what it takes to break free of any fears or negativity that has been holding you back. You are ready. And if you don't think you are, remember that no one, not even Beyonce, feels ready. We are all figuring life out. We're all figuring out love. We're all figuring out relationships. We're all figuring out who we are.

Confidence and Courage

If you wait until you feel ready, you may be waiting for your entire life. You can find courage when you step into your confident warrior. She's got your back and will

49

provide you with all the courage that you need. No matter how shitty things get, she is the one person you can always count on.

She fights the negative beliefs and thoughts that influence your worth and confidence. She's never going to abandon you. She's that voice in the back of your head that quietly tells you, "You're too worthy of feeding yourself negative thoughts, girl!"

Trust me; I've doubted my confident warrior plenty of times. Still, that girl came through when I had nowhere else to go. It was shortly after my breakup with Jake that I felt way down. Even though I felt euphoria leaving that relationship, I had moments of:

"Can I actually get through this?"

"Will I ever find a man who can treat me the way I love myself on the inside?"

That answer was a hell yeah, Carla! Since then, I've had relationships with men that prove my confident warrior had my back.

The confident warrior has been with you all along. It may feel like a completely new thing that's happening because you've never experienced growth or true confidence like this before.

So many people live their lives, telling themselves the same story repeatedly. Congratulations! You're ready to let go of your old story and step into your fully confident, unstoppable, and unapologetic self.

It's ok if your legs are shaking and you feel like you can hardly stand. You can. You can always stand tall and step into this. Recognizing you have something to say gives you strength and courage as you take ownership of your choices in relationships, dating, and breakups.

Watch the Confidence Grow

For me, this confidence came as I was going through that toxic breakup with Jake. To this day, I can feel that pit in my stomach. Looking back, I felt trapped. I felt like there was no way out except to make the relationship work. I struggled to stand.

I like to say that I was being tested. My Higher Power put this relationship in my life because it was necessary. Everything that occurs in your life is necessary. The good. The bad. The happy. The sad. It's what you do with it that allows you to live a life you choose fully.

I kept playing back and forth with this confident warrior inside of me. I felt her creep up, yet I would push her down. I was afraid to let go of the past as it had protected me and kept me small. I felt comfortable playing small. It validated the relationships I chose to be in.

It wasn't until a sunny April 2nd in LA that I knew I was deserving. When Jake picked me up at the airport from my trip to Ireland, I knew I loved myself too much to be with him. I was too powerful to continue being treated this way. Those thoughts forced me into taking action. This moment literally brought me to my knees. I finally made a choice that put me first.

It felt damn good as I officially ended things with Jake. As I approached his house one last time, I knew I was irreplaceable, unstoppable, bold, and fierce—assets that could get through some heavy shit.

I felt empowered. I no longer had to stay and play the victim over and over again. My confident warrior shielded me with self-worth and self-love. I knew I was going to be ok as I was taking care of myself.

I knew I didn't have to play out this old story in my head—the one that validated these codependent relationships. I was finally letting that shit go. I stepped into my confident warrior knowing there was no going back. I wasn't alone. I always had me. I just had to reach inside and pull out the strength.

I won. Nothing and nobody could ever hold that power over me again. Inside me is a confident warrior. And that badass, well, she's never going anywhere. Just as my confident warrior led me through growth and change, yours will too. So, how do you tap into this shit? I've got you covered with these five steps.

Five Steps to Accessing Your Confident Warrior

1. Figure out what you want.

Sometimes we think we know what we want but choose out of fear. Or maybe we've been told what to do for so many years that we begin believing it, and feel that it's our only option. Often, we use our default button because it makes us feel most comfortable, but we don't realize how much it isolates us from others. Other times you can't hear the confident warrior because you aren't familiar with her voice and don't know she's there.

Elle was vibrant, ambitious as hell and felt the need to make her relationship with her boyfriend work. She thought she wanted to be in a relationship, but her actions suggested otherwise. Her finances suffered because Elle picked up her boyfriend's financial slack due to his irresponsible spending habits. She was afraid that if she let go, she would lose herself.

I asked her to make a list of the things that she wanted in a relationship. She listed: to feel safe, have healthy communication, trust, mutual love, and independence. We then compared what was really going on in her relationship: being the only one putting effort into the relationship, feeling responsible for his finances, not trusting him as a result of his inconsistency, feeling like she had to earn his love, and buying into his victimhood. This became a major reality check. Elle had nothing she wanted in the relationship and was only hanging on out of fear.

Sometimes we don't want to face the reality of what we truly want due to our feelings of failure, shame, guilt, and fear. When you have your confident warrior by your side, you won't have to go through these emotions alone. Lean on her to guide you in figuring out what you want, not the narrative of "this will get better" or "he briefly stopped drinking so he's trying." This helps shift you into a space of making decisions and choices based on what you want versus what someone else wants.

2. Decide to move forward.

There is a big misconception that if you know what you want, then you should go after it. The problem is with the word *should*. You're never going to go after a change unless you want it damn bad.

Emma wanted her husband to stop drinking. He repeatedly told her he would stop. He seemed genuine, and she believed him. Every time he'd pick up the bottle again, she felt helpless, frustrated, and let down. Eventually, Emma realized her husband had to want to change. It wasn't her responsibility to make him change. She had no control over his choices.

As a result, she focused on herself, the things she could change, instead of her husband's drinking. She began going to brunch with girlfriends and joined a running club. She created a life for herself. She was no longer afraid to go out and do things because her husband may drink.

Her husband continued to drink, but her feelings shifted. Emma allowed him to take responsibility for his problem, which allowed her to focus on creating a life where she didn't feel restricted. When you figure out what you want, then you can decide how you want to move forward. It's a change in mindset. You're taking back control of your life.

3. Make a commitment to yourself.

The word commitment can feel daunting. If you're like me, you've probably put pressure on yourself thinking it's an all or nothing situation—AKA, a big fucking deal. When you break down the actual definition of commitment, (thanks, Google), it means 1. the state or quality of being dedicated to a cause, activity, etc.

This definition tells me it is only about dedicating yourself to something. It doesn't mean you have to put black warrior paint under your eyes and go into battle. When you make a commitment to yourself, you're creating the relationship between you and what you want. You mandate the rules. There is no one telling you how to make a commitment to yourself and what it should look like but you.

As she says, Mia was single as a Pringle. She got out of a codependent relationship three years prior, decided she wanted to date again and was ready to move forward. She was confused about how much time and effort to put into dating. She had some fears about dating someone with a mental illness who wasn't taking care of himself. She wasn't sure if she felt ready to dive right into dating.

I told her to put her toe in the water. She didn't need to jump in fully. I explained she could put her feet in and eventually do some warm-up laps. As this felt manageable to her, she decided that if she committed little by little, she could do it.

Committing to yourself is very personal. You don't need to tell the world, let alone post to social media. Honor your damn preciousness during this time as this a huge flipping deal. Get ready to take life into your own hands. You don't need to set this commitment in stone, but it's essential to make sure you can firmly take it on.

4. Act on it.

The only way for change to truly occur is to take action. Doing so can be terrifying, scary, or exciting. It's time to make some moves, girl! Sometimes inaction is action. Sometimes saying no to your loved one or someone who asks a favor is action.

Colleen decided not to date for two months, which meant saying no to potential dates and not pursuing the dating apps. She felt that being in a relationship gave her validation. So, instead, she decided to call a time out and work on validating herself.

Was this easy for her? Hell no. Colleen wanted to date. However, she was nervous that dating would break her commitment to herself. She knew her old ways were no longer working, and she was ready to try something that could work.

Meanwhile, Colleen took action in how she was interacting with her partner. Instead of allowing him to take charge of a situation, she decided to speak up when she felt unsatisfied. Doing this helped Colleen feel empowered and was a way to show her thoughts and opinions mattered.

Taking action does not mean stressing yourself out to the point of insanity. In the simplest terms, it means making a conscious decision to move forward. It's much easier said than done. At first, you may even back out of wanting to do it, or maybe you're so eager you overdo it. Keep in mind that your confident warrior is in your corner. You can pull tools from her toolbox if you're feeling a bit stressed at this stage. Trust that she will never put you in a position that you can't grow in.

5. Embrace your fuck up: recognize you're not perfect.

Remember, you are not alone. You can access this confident warrior at any time. Because of this awareness, you can't go back. You know too much about your worth.

Kristy had been working with me for about six sessions. During her seventh session, she said, "I thought about lying to you and only disclosing a little of the story, but I decided to grow through this fully, I needed to be honest with you." She took a deep breath and continued, "I feel like I didn't honor myself. I wanted so badly to create the boundary between me and my ex, James. Instead, I covered for his behavior this past weekend with my family at dinner."

Kristy had invited James to a family dinner. Even though she had been trying to distance herself from him, she wanted to include him. At dinner, everyone was enjoying their meal. James leaned over and complained to Kristy that the food sucked, and he was going to write a bad Yelp review. She begged him not to do anything. Her brother chose the restaurant, was paying, and as a result, Kristy felt responsible for his actions.

The next morning, she got a call from her brother, who saw James' scathing Yelp review. Immediately she began to blame herself. I asked her what she learned from this experience. She paused for about one minute. Like one long-ass pause—that pause someone takes when they're doing that inner work deep thinking shit. "I learned that this is a major red flag, which is something I would never have known if it weren't for working with you."

Easy Access to the Confident Warrior

Just like Kristy, none of us are perfect, damn it! It's progress, not perfection. I always need to remind myself of this. I can be so hard on the expectations I put on myself. I set them too high and then become my own worst critic when I can't achieve the high expectations I've set.

The beauty of the confident warrior is she's still there. She still loves you after your imperfection hits a wall. The confident warrior is always available. Sometimes you might think she has left, but she hasn't. Just reach in and call for her. She will lead you to true change.

The confident warrior can teach you the damn hard practice of recognizing red flags while being gentle with yourself. Watch for those red flags, girl. Sometimes they are hard to see and leave you with fuzzy vision. The confident warrior has your back as she guides you. Put on those Warby Parker glasses and start seeing those red flags in 20/20 vision.

 Damn Good Affirmation: #IAmUnstoppable

 How can you tap into your confident warrior?

DODGE THOSE RED FLAGS

What the hell are red flags, anyways? I once asked, "There are actually warning signs when someone is a psycho out there?" Huh. Who knew! Certainly not me as I sat in my therapist's office working through another codependent relationship.

I had never heard of red flags before. Now I realized how many red flags I missed in my past relationships. Time and time again, I ignored them even though my gut told me something was wrong. I just wanted the relationship to work out.

And this girl (me) was painting red flags green.

My old love life pattern kinda went like this:

1. I love the feeling of dating someone new. Oh hello, relationship high!
2. All my insecurities feel like they peaced out and left for good.
3. The feeling of "you'll be single forever" vanishes as I've received the ultimate badge of self-worth and self-love validation from the person I'm dating. Finally, someone likes me and is paying attention to me!

Disclaimer: Don't be that girl! Trust in your confident warrior, and you'll have a foundation of self-love and trust in your corner. If you don't, you will be waiting a long time for another person to justify your worth, and when I say a long time, I mean forever.

Follow Your Damn Gut Already

When I first went on a date with Jake, he talked all about the fancy Porsches he drove and provided details about breakups with his exes. Did it feel off? Very. It's my gut saying, "Carla, wake the fuck up." If something feels off, it probably is.

For most of us, when it comes to red flags, we convince ourselves into what I call a logic mind fuck. You might justify the behavior of this person, put them on a pedestal, make excuses for them, keep information about them hidden from friends and family, change our schedule to meet their needs or keep seeing them when you know it doesn't feel right. Your number one red flag indicator is when your gut tells you something is off.

Consider your gut your BFF for life. While it's one of the most complex relationships you're going to have, it's usually right. It's only looking out for you. Get to know her and be loyal. The more we ignore these red flags and spray green washable ink over them we realize the joke is on us.

Eventually, the flag turns neon and grows so high that we can't hide from it or stuff it down. When we try to do that it only surfaces bigger each time, follow your damn gut! If it ain't right, girl, it ain't right.

Recognizing Red Flags

Flags come in all shapes in sizes. That's why it can feel confusing as hell to sort through them. If you're looking for red flags instead of allowing a relationship or date to evolve naturally, you may miss the real one. It's kind of like putting together a puzzle with a missing a piece. You have zero control over ever finding that piece because it's not there, yet you continue to look.

If you become so focused on your red flag checklist, you're no longer going to be present. You'll only be looking to check off those boxes. When you're not present, it inhibits your ability to tap into your gut. You learn lessons when you don't follow your gut. Chelsey went on a few dates with a new guy. After three dates, he told her he couldn't make time to see her but wanted to text and talk on the phone every night. I noted these might be red flags. This guy was emotionally unavailable to see her in person but wanted constant communication.

After a few weeks, checking to see if he called or texted her consumed her. One night, she told him she was a writer. He asked to read some of her work. She sent him an editorial about family dynamics. Thirty minutes later, he responded with a very long emotional text. In this text, he projected his entire relationship with his mom on to her.

He told her he couldn't be with someone who didn't have a strong family connection. He needed someone who had that because he didn't. I could sit here and go into psychoanalyzing his issues, but first, I'm not a therapist and second, it's not about him, it's about my client.

She felt abandoned by this guy and recognized he

hadn't actively worked on himself. As a result of working together, she knew this was a major red flag, and she needed someone who had done self-work. I told her that God's rejection is God's protection. In reality, her Higher Power was working for her, not against her. Whether she recognized the red flags or not, she was not supposed to be with this person.

As a result of that long-winded text, Chelsey said she didn't want to speak to him again and blocked him on her phone. She didn't want to be triggered by inappropriate texts from him. The next day he wrote her a long text and led with, "I know you blocked me, but I wanted to reach out via Google voice text." He continued saying how sorry he was for what he did and that he took it too far. She didn't respond to him but thought real hard on his text.

She told me it would be ok if he waited a few weeks to text her but now was too soon. And I said, "Either way he's not respecting your boundaries. If you block him and he finds another way to reach out, that's a red flag. It's no longer about you. Instead, he makes it about him needing to reach out."

The Thing About Red Flags

Red flags are twofold: the bigger, more significant, issue and the symptoms. The symptom is the result of the action while the bigger issue is what's really going on inside. For example, a compulsive gambler may not have enough money to pay for their date's coffee. That's the symptom.

Meanwhile, the bigger issue is their gambling problem. There are also more subtle symptoms or clues not directly correlated to the addiction. These could include being rude to wait staff, not wanting to fully commit to a relationship, not wanting to meet friends, bashing their ex, or having no friends. It's like standing on Malibu Beach looking out at the water and seeing what's on the surface but never seeing the creatures that live on the bottom.

When we think of someone not having their shit together, it's all about the big stuff. For example, a lot of people think of an addict as someone who sits on the street corner begging for money. Lots of addicts function normally in day to day life and have careers.

So, this is tricky. Most addicts are functioning people. When Claudia first started dating her boyfriend Eric, he was going through some financial troubles. He had been living with his ex-girlfriend, and when they broke up, he had a hard time affording rent on his own. While looking for a place to live, Eric moved into the back office where he worked for a month. Claudia justified his story because he needed to find a place where he could keep his dog.

Eventually, Eric got approved for housing and moved into his own place. After a year of dating, they moved in together. Claudia is an awesome go-getter. At the time, she was 26 and making $90k per year working in corporate. Her finances were buttoned up. Around tax season she noticed Eric wasn't filing his taxes and wasn't requesting an extension either. This made her anxious and wasn't the only red flag she saw. Before this, Eric had started collecting money under the table from his personal training clients. He hid thousands of dollars under his nightstand.

When she asked him about it, he got very defensive. Her gut felt off, but she didn't act on it. Eventually, Eric admitted he hadn't filed taxes for two years. He thought he could "slip under the rug." She felt paralyzed. She knew how smart he was and that he loved her, and she loved him.

She felt torn knowing that if the relationship continued, she could be responsible for IRS audits. That was a lot of financial responsibility she didn't want to take on. She didn't want to break up either. She went back and forth on what to do because she saw the potential in him and the relationship.

Over time, shit started to happen. Eric's car got towed, and he had a screaming fit and took off his shoes and threw them across the street. When he came back inside the apartment, he apologized to the dog, but not Claudia. In shock, Claudia said, "Don't I get an apology?" Eric shrugged and said, "I wasn't ready, but I'm sorry." And again, her gut was screaming at her.

A week later, Claudia came home from work ready to enjoy a peaceful Wednesday night to herself. When she walked in the door, Eric immediately said he wanted to break up with her. When he realized they weren't right for one another, she was pissed and felt betrayed. Meanwhile, her gut knew it was the right thing. She didn't try to reason with him or reject the breakup. Instead, she packed her belongings, got the fuck out of the apartment, and worked on a relationship with herself.

Shortly after, Claudia changed careers, got her own apartment, and found herself. After our last session, she was the happiest she had ever been in her life. Claudia was fully living for herself. If she hadn't followed her gut and got out of the relationship, things could have gotten messier. Eric was in severe debt and in potential trouble with the IRS. Claudia didn't realize the extent of the troubles until the end of the relationship and didn't pay attention to the red flags right from the start.

Watch out for these common red flag symptoms:

- Talks about their ex in a negative way
- Doesn't communicate back consistently and "disappears" then suddenly comes back
- Discloses very personal family issues or personal issues they're currently going through
- Rude to the wait staff
- Can't commit to seeing you
- Saying one thing but you observe their behavior doing something else
- Shows up late to things
- Their words speak louder than their actions
- No interest in meeting your friends or doesn't introduce you to theirs
- Gets angry over simple conflict or disagreement
- Can't connect sexually
- Pressures you sexually
- Doesn't seem to have a secure living situation
- Hot and cold mood leaving you walking on eggshells
- Leaves bills for you to pay in full
- Only wants to hang out when they feel like it

- Checks in on you and who you're with frequently
- Conflict causes high emotions
- Personality changes with drinking or drugs

Recognizing red flags and honoring when something feels off empowers you to choose your relationship status or date. No matter what your relationship status is, it's essential to focus on yourself. Claudia saw that she could have issues with the IRS or have to be financially responsible for a future apartment.

Typically, when you're first starting to date somebody or getting to know your current partner better, the symptoms of bigger issues begin to surface. They aren't always easy to spot. That's why it's super important to check in with yourself if you feel off. When triggered by something that makes you angry or embarrassed, to gain more clarity, talk it over with a trusted friend or write down exactly what happened. By doing so, you can see a situation with more clarity. This allows you to focus on the issue instead of brushing it under the rug.

For Claudia, her initial red flag was Eric needing to move into his work's back office. She couldn't see the bigger picture of reasons why he wasn't paying his taxes. Sometimes it's easier to see the big picture played out after you get to know this person. That's when all the symptoms come together to make sense.

When you start dating someone, and you don't have the answers for the bigger issue, the symptoms can feel confusing. Especially if you were anything like me and had no fucking clue what symptoms looked like. Or maybe you fell so hard and felt so fucked over by someone that you can't trust yourself to spot your symptoms. You may find yourself always wondering if something they said or did was a symptom.

Breathe. I've got you.

If you're in a codependent relationship or you're dating someone who is, you can totally feel hazy. You may really love this person and not understand why you keep feeling like everything you're doing for the relationship isn't working. The best thing you can do is check in with yourself and have a serious, honest conversation within. By not doing so, you continue running a marathon with no end. You'll become exhausted and eventually lose your footing.

The relationship will have no boundaries, and you'll find yourself mixed up with the other person's problem or emotions. This is a perfect place for codependency to harvest and grow into an unwanted, unhealthy relationship. All you have control over is your part. That's it. You're not superwoman.

No matter how hard you try to change yourself to be the perfect partner, no matter how much you try to show this person how to fix their problem, no matter how hard you justify their symptom or more significant issue, you can't solve it. You've got to face the reality that it's the end of the night. The bar has closed, and the lights have turned on. At that moment, you see everyone exactly as they are. Allow your gut to guide you through the dimmed light so that it leads you into full light.

Gut Check-In

How do you check-in with yourself? Listen to that gut. Unfortunately, sometimes *what you want* isn't the same as *what you feel*. Listen to *what you feel* rather than *what you want*. It's in there. It's deep within. It's part of the confident warrior nudging you into your worth and looking out for you. When you get out of your own way, you can step into happiness.

One thing you can truly count on is your gut. With codependency, you might feel like you should ignore your gut because you know how to "fix" this person's problem. In truth, the only thing that can help relieve the situation is figuring out what the hell you want knowing this person isn't going to cure their own red flags magically.

It's time to unmask the symptoms and bigger issues. You can even analyze and talk to friends about this person and what they need. Trying to solve why they acted this way in the first place will get you nowhere. When you focus on the other person, you're really doing yourself a huge disservice. You have to focus on you.

Kayla was having a hard time with dating. She never had a serious boyfriend so wasn't exactly sure what was normal or what she wanted. She met Patrick on a business trip. He was smart and in the process of getting his Ph.D. All was good until some red flags showed up.

He told her that a woman he worked with was annoying and he would insult her until she walked away. Patrick also mentioned his friend Dan didn't invite him to a basketball game which pissed him off. In return, he cut Dan off and chose not to speak to him again. Listening to her gut, Kayla worried that if they continued seeing one another these symptoms would affect their relationship.

TBH, kudos to Kayla cause yeah they absolutely would.

Kayla wanted to make the situation better by helping Patrick. I asked her to focus on herself instead of making her boyfriend's situation a priority. She agreed but didn't know what that would look like or where to begin.

Together we focused on why these symptoms made her feel uncomfortable. As Patrick so easily cut people out of his life. She was afraid he'd do that to her. And then there was the instance of insulting someone to the point of harassment. From there, we pinpointed what she truly wanted in a partner. She soon realized what she was "settling" into with Patrick.

After we finished our session, Kayla looked at me and smiled, "You know, I'm too valuable to waste my time with someone who doesn't match what I want. And ultimately, yes, I want a relationship, but I will waste more time if I enter the wrong relationship than if I hold out in the unknown of being single waiting for the relationship I want to be in."

Don't ignore the red flags. You can choose to see them or not. It's up to you to decide. Follow your damn gut.

The symptoms will always surface. If it feels off, it doesn't mean you have to stick around for the big issue. No matter how much you try to justify in your mind that the symptoms are not that bad, there is always a big issue at the root of it all. Unless this person has shown that they are actively working on their big issue, then assume nothing will change.

To spot red flags, you need to create some boundaries. These boundaries will keep you afloat and help you focus on what you need when things aren't working for you. In the next chapter, you'll see how boundaries can provide a sense of self-structure and accountability.

Damn Good Advice: It is ok to throw up your white flag. Trust me. There are plenty of green flags in the field.

 Damn Good Affirmation: #MyGutGuidesMe

 What red flags have you noticed or pushed away in your relationships or dating life?

CHAPTER 6

HOW TO BUILD BOUNDARIES FOR DAMN GOOD

Boundaries are the lifeline to being a damn good independent badass. K, cool story. But what exactly are boundaries and why do they matter? They keep your relationships, dating life, and breakups from becoming an emotional cluster fuck. It gives you purpose and a voice in self-worth and self-love. It's the bloodline to breaking free from contagious love.

Boundaries set limits and give you independence. Boundaries define how far you're truly willing to go for someone in a relationship or the person you're dating. They help you step into what's best for you. And yes, you can still:

- Love someone and look out for yourself first.
- Date someone and put your needs first.
- Take care of yourself in the haze of a breakup.

You need to look inward. Creating boundaries involves being direct, taking into consideration self-care, speaking up, and sticking to your decision. For example, Kendall and her husband Laurence would get in intense arguments that went well into the middle of the night. The next day, she'd be too tired to focus at work. She set a conflict discussion cut-off time with Lawrence to ensure the late

71

arguments weren't keeping her up all night.

She told Laurence that at 7:45 pm they needed to stop any conflict and resume discussing it the next day. Laurence respected the boundary, and they practiced it effectively twice. The third time, he tried to push the boundary, Kendall began to engage with him and then stopped herself because she wanted to honor her needs first.

Disclaimer: The good news is the boundaries you set in your romantic relationships can apply to work, family, and friendships too.

Putting yourself first can seem like a bizarre idea. Focusing on your damn self may feel overwhelming. Creating your own space may feel like you're alone and sinking in the middle of the ocean.

If you've spent a lot of emotional time looking out for this other person, it can feel like you're abandoning them. It can also feel awkward because you're peacing out on them. Maybe you don't want to leave what you've worked so hard to put together. Even if you aren't with them currently, you probably still have emotional ties and connection. Stalking their Instagram or Facebook and seeing what they're "up to" is a boundary violation. A healthy boundary includes not stalking your ex on social media.

Disclaimer: We're all guilty of searching our exes profiles every once in a while.

Boundaries are the Secret Sauce

If you want your future or current relationships to thrive, then boundaries are the Domino Confectioners vanilla buttercream frosting to your Pillsbury Funfetti cake, girl. The two go together perfectly. You need that buttercream frosting for your future or current relationships. *Side note: this is my birthday cake every year.*

It's time to decide whether you want to continue sitting in a space where you feel comfortable, but aren't contributing to the actual relationship in a positive way or if you're going to step into owning your part by setting boundaries. I'm just going to be real with you, sister. If you don't set boundaries, you will not progress from breaking free and stepping into your damn good self. Don't let inner fear and thoughts of the unknown stop you from doing what's best for you.

Not long ago, I did not understand the concept of boundaries. I thought if I gave everything in my relationships and went to crazy extremes to show them that I was there for them, then that was love. That's not love. Before my personal growth and self-love journey, Jake needed to get surgery. I can't say he was a narcissist because that's not my place, but he was abusive and made everything about him. He put himself above everything and everyone.

He made such a big deal of this surgery that I got wrapped into being his sole caretaker. There was a part of me that felt special to be the one by his hospital bedside, helping him shower and taking days off work to be there for him. Mind you; I had only been dating him for five months.

I wanted him to see how much I loved him. These actions equaled love in my mind.

I gave everything but wasn't getting anything in return. Jake got frustrated when I took a night off to be by myself. I felt guilty when he gave me a hard time. He blamed me for not fully showing up. So, I kept giving him everything *he* needed. Eventually, when he recovered from the surgery, I had no sense of self in the relationship.

Things only got worse over time. I felt it was my responsibility to show him how much I cared, so I would get care in return. However, the more I pushed, the more the relationship became toxic. As a result, I felt isolated, confused, and alone. But, I wasn't ready to throw in the towel yet.

I was at war with my ego. I couldn't get someone to love me the way I needed so I stuck around way past the expiration date. When I tried to leave and breakup, Jake promised me he'd change. I fell into this cycle in all my relationships.

It came to a halt when I couldn't take it anymore. Jake was gaslighting me, and when it finally did end, he wouldn't leave me the fuck alone.

Disclaimer: According to Google, gaslighting means to "manipulate (someone) by psychological means into questioning their own sanity."

After I blocked Jake, he:

- Posted a manipulative Facebook status about how much he loved me so friends would reach out.
- Used somebody else's phone number to call me.
- Emailed me from a different email address.
- Emailed my closest friends long messages about how much our relationship meant to him.

In the end, I went to the police station, with my two roommates there for support, to see what my legal options were regarding harassment. I created my first boundary by taking steps to break up with him and by committing to follow through.

Ah-ha moment: I made choices that best suited my needs, not what *he* wanted or expected from me.

The best conversation and reasoning you can have with an abuser is zero communication. For the first time in my life, I was creating boundaries, standing up, and respecting myself. If I didn't get my shit together and incorporate or include boundaries, I realized I'd be on a continuous slippery slope trying to run backward uphill. Let's be real, that's freakin' impossible. Once you start sliding down, it's serious work to get back to where you were.

Time travel forward—today, I create boundaries in every relationship. Do I do it perfectly? No, because I'm human. But today, I understand why I need to create boundaries. In my past relationships, I went through the boundary crash so I could have the gift of owning who I am. As a result, today, I have a sense of self in relationships.

It didn't come overnight. It wasn't like boom—I was boundary mother fucking kween. No, it took time and practice. It involved checking in and growing the relationship within before I knew what my boundaries were. The more you practice it, the more damn good and confident you feel. It's a beautiful thing, but it's a process. There is no quick fix. All you can do is take it a day and sometimes a moment at a time.

When creating boundaries, commit to putting yourself first, checking-in with yourself, promising not to follow red flag dudes, and breaking things off in a toxic relationship even if that relationship has some promise.

Creating boundaries ain't easy, but neither is being in codependent relationships that repeatedly break you down. Now, you get to decide how you want to create boundaries. Truthfully, only you know what's right. No one is going to give you a sparkly wand and say, "Bam, motherfucker, that's it." When it comes to creating boundaries, these three simple steps are your sparkle.

Three Steps to Doing You

1. Be your own gym buddy. You're the only person who's going to be able to say, "Get the hell up; it's time for your workout class," AKA keep yourself accountable and have your own back. You've gotta wake the hell up because it's time to start making moves. It doesn't have to be an elaborate dance piece. Hell, it can be the ugliest sidestep you've ever done, but the idea is that you do it. It's time to commit to what you need to do to look out for yourself. The second you decide to stop moving, you're fucked. So, whatever you do, move those damn feet of yours to create those appropriate boundaries.

Katherine's boyfriend Diego wanted to move in with her, but there were some red flags. She loved him, but something felt off. She had been avoiding talking about moving in together because she was afraid to upset him. Katherine felt like she was walking on eggshells around him.

I reminded her that she had options, and it wasn't always about what he wanted. By avoiding the conversation, she was doing a disservice to herself. It wasn't really about upsetting Diego; it was about making choices for herself.

Eventually, Katherine decided to be direct with Diego. She chose to talk about it after watching an episode on Netflix from *Schitt's Creek* because the air in the room would be lighter. She said, "Diego, I love you and care a lot about you. I know we have discussed moving in together, but I need more time of living alone." Diego was a bit taken back but ultimately respected that she felt this way. And as a result, Katherine felt more confident and in control of her part in the relationship.

2. Create space to gain your damn vocal cords back.
Not having boundaries is like trying to sing after Julie Andrews, the OG of *The Sound of Music*, and have vocal cord surgery. It's impossible and dangerous to your health.

If you're currently in a codependent relationship, open that mouth of yours and own your part in the relationship. If you're not feeling comfortable with the way your partner is treating you or themselves, you get to create the opportunity to step aside from controlling their behavior. Control can look like telling them they need to get therapy, stop drinking, or taking on their financial responsibilities. It begins by saying no to favors that make you feel uncomfortable.

After a breakup, you get to decide if you want to be friends with your ex. People love to gossip during a breakup. But, you don't have to be the center of their circus. It's not your monkeys, and it's not your circus. No matter how much you still feel connected to this person, after the breakup you're not together. You need to create your own space. If you suspect your ex will be showing up at an event or party, don't go for mental health reasons. This is not about being antisocial; it is literally about taking care of yourself.

If you're currently dating someone and it's an unhealthy relationship, you get to decide whether you want to move forward or not. If they're not respecting your space, you can create boundaries and say how you're feeling. You can walk away if you see red flags.

You have options, girl! You're not helpless. But, it's up to you to open your eyes for your own damn good.

3. Be firm with yourself. Logic is not your friend. I don't care how many grids you pull out to make an analytical case for why you shouldn't continue your boundary. It's time for some tough love. It's easy to say, "This is too much. Screw the boundaries, and I'll figure it out myself."

Disclaimer: Your best thinking is what got you to this place.

You don't have to do boundaries perfectly. If you seek perfection, then you'll always be searching for the next best thing. All you need is progress. If you don't follow through on a boundary, it's ok. You don't need to beat yourself up.

Sometimes it takes a couple of tries or maybe some back and forth in your mind until you truly feel ready to create that boundary. It's time to step up your game. It's easy to slip back into old behaviors. Never forget that you always have the option to start your day over at any given moment.

I met Ryan shortly after I broke things off with Jake and began my self-love and self-growth journey. I approached him out with friends one night. He was from Nebraska living in Los Angeles, and something charming about his Midwest friendliness—something I wasn't used to as I was an East Coast girl at heart.

I knew I needed to do more work on myself rather than date someone new. My gut was roaring. I so badly wanted to ignore my gut feeling and keep seeing Ryan. But I knew I couldn't. While there was this magnetic force, I knew something was off.

I had to keep a promise to myself. If I wanted to step into my journey, I needed to do it without being in a relationship. I needed to learn who I truly was. I felt like I was standing with one foot in the water of self-love and growth and another foot in the fire of the past. It was a sign from my Higher Power that I have a choice. When I am tempted to abandon myself, I know I always have options on how to move forward.

I followed my gut and let this thing with Ryan go. I kept it short and simple, letting him know we couldn't have a relationship. He protested, but I didn't settle or buy into that narrative.

In truth, I didn't know who or what I was going to be once I spent time with myself. However, I knew I needed to protect and honor the crap out of myself. Thank God I listened to that gut of mine. I love who I am today. I can tell you 24-year-old Carla is worth it.

The Power of Boundaries

Often overlooked, boundaries are an insanely powerful force. They give you a sense of self—your own identity. If you act on them, they can save your life. Boundaries aren't only for leaving an abusive relationship. In my case, setting boundaries saved my life from living for other people. I learned what I truly wanted, how I wanted to speak my truth, the power it takes to create my happiness, and how to put myself first when it comes to my wants and needs.

When you start speaking your truth, you find your voice. This is something that took me a long while to learn how to do, but I eventually landed it. How do you push past the discomfort of people-pleasing, fear, worry, shame, guilt to fully own your voice? I cover that in the next chapter.

Damn Good Affirmation: #IAmEnough

 Create one boundary you'd like to practice this week and explain how you will do it.

FIND YOUR DAMN VOICE

It's time to stop being quiet and start making noise. It's time to feel damn good! You've been holding back for way too damn long, girl! Let's stop this going back and forth, questioning whether you are going to be your true authentic self or whether you want to try to fit in *his* life. Instead, ask yourself, "Is *he* going to fit in my life?" That's a pretty big shift in thinking.

You're too valuable to abandon your thoughts, emotions, and not pay attention to your gut. So, how do you achieve it? Communication is your number one go-getter. Without communication, your inner emotions and thoughts fall flat. Trust me. Been there, done that.

My gut knew it was time to speak up when I became aware that something just wasn't right. Did I feel scared? Yup. Did I question if I was overreacting? Yup. Did I have a hard time trusting myself that this was right? Yup. And I see the same type of blocks surface for my clients who want to find their voice when it comes to relationships. By keeping it simple, you too can let those inner vocals shine.

Stand Up for What's Right

For the first time, you can begin standing up for yourself because you now have boundaries. Now, you have the desire to figure your shit out. If you're having trouble finding your voice for the first time, rely on your confident warrior to support you. Most likely, you'll feel uncomfortable. Well, hell, anytime you're doing something for yourself for the first time or doing something that means a lot to you—you'll feel the discomfort. Nobody has ever died from being uncomfortable. It's true.

When you have self-love, you see your worth and recognize the red flags. At this point, you know where your boundaries lie, and you're not going to sit back and tolerate somebody doing something unacceptable to you. I'm not saying to use your voice to control somebody else's behavior or tell them everything they're doing wrong. Instead, I'm asking you to focus 110 percent on yourself.

By not focusing on yourself, you'll get tangled back up into codependency. By doing so, you are throwing your boundaries, red flags, your self-love, and worse out the window. Am I saying you are going to be able to speak your truth every single time? No. Life continues to happen. New situations and scenarios happen, but that's what growth is all about. Consider using your voice to be just one extra tool that you can use to stay true to who you are. And if you don't do this perfectly, then you're doing it right. The more you push against your gut, the more you're doing a disservice to your self-love.

In a way, awareness is your new best friend. You no longer need to question certain things. Your intuitive or gut feeling is not going to let you fall back into those old behavior patterns. You may get tripped up, stumble, or fall here and there. But you never have to go back 100 percent to how it was before.

You have a choice. You get to decide. You can ask, "Do I speak my truth? Do I speak up? Do I act on these boundaries? Do I act on the red flags? Do I act on my self-love and self-worth?" Yes. Yes, you do. You are too valuable and too worthy to stay quiet and be held back by the illusions we call fear. It's these blocks that have been telling you you're something you're not. The most important thing that you can do is trust yourself and use your voice.

Speak Your Truth

Alright, so let's be clear here. You're at a point where maybe you're scared AF. Ok, I got it. But you're going to speak your truth anyway because it's important to you. And you want healthy intimate relationships. I'm just going to break it to you. If you don't speak your truth, you will not get the results that you want when it comes to intimacy.

Other blocks sometimes get in the way of speaking up. Usually, we know deep within us what those blocks are. One big block could be not wanting to officially end things with an ex because the attention and validation that they still care about you lingers. Or maybe it's telling that dude you went out with on a not so great date that you're not interested because you saw some big red flags. Somehow, you keep talking to him and avoid telling him *no* because you are a people pleaser and are afraid to upset him. Or maybe you're wanting to avoid that conversation with your partner because you know deep within speaking up for yourself is no longer playing by his rules. You may feel you are putting yourself in a position where you know there could be consequences to having him feel a certain way about you. And when you speak up, it can feel intimidating, putting yourself out there and expressing your needs.

Elaine is a 28-year-old chick living in NYC. She sought therapy when she was sexually assaulted in college to help get through the trauma. When she came to work with me, she was having trouble speaking her truth on dates. She didn't know how to discuss the past because she had been in codependent relationships or relationships where she felt "comfortable."

She was a passionate person with an all or nothing personality that bled onto her dates. She would either overshare or under share to protect herself. When she overshared, it would create a mish-mosh of boundaries and, when she under shared, she couldn't connect with her dates. Dating and relationships left her exhausted and confused.

When I asked her what stopped her from speaking her truth, she replied, "I've never felt that I was respected enough, and I got tired of guys giving me a hard time. Sometimes it's easier to keep going along than to stop." She said she had no criteria for turning down dates. I replied, "What are the things that bring you the feeling of joy and safety?" She easily listed off a few and ended with, "Ultimately, being around friends that I trust makes me happy."

I encouraged her to speak her truth the next time she didn't want to date someone any longer. I encouraged her to have a safety plan in place that brings her joy, such as meeting a girlfriend for some matcha. As we spoke, she said she felt as if she gained clarity. She realized she was doing a disservice to not only the guys but to herself by not speaking her truth. Speaking your truth is a form of self-care and self-love. Having a plan made Elaine feel safe. She knows she has tools to speak her truth, own her truth, and practice it with some self-care.

It Takes Two to Tango

In relationships, we often want the other person to be satisfied and happy that we totally neglect the other 50 percent. What's the other 50 percent? YOU. You're doing any relationship a huge disservice if you don't figure out what you need and act on it. It truly does take two to tango.

Communication is everything when it comes to relationships. We first learn to communicate by watching our parents talk to one another or even talk to us. From there, we take on this learned behavior. We're never really taught what proper communication is. You go to school, study, learn math, learn how to read, and how to write (although sometimes I still wonder if my grammar is ok and I can't believe I'm writing a book, but I digress). Yet, nobody is giving us the most important lesson of all time—effective communication.

Once you figure out what it is you want and need, then it's time to place that into words. It can feel uncomfortable because confrontation is not easy when you are speaking your truth. I can tell you this, talking through the discomfort is more beneficial to you than holding back.

Use Your Voice

Let's start with this. Find your damn voice. When

you're feeling upset or wanting to set a boundary, keep the focus only on yourself, use your voice. When you open your mouth and begin to blame the other person and tell them they are doing something wrong—stop! That creates immediate blame and honestly shows you're not allowing them the space to take ownership for their part.

Be gentle. While you can communicate in anger by asserting that someone has wronged you, take responsibility for only what you have control over. This can be difficult, especially if you feel that the person totally fucked you over or is being rude. You're the only person who can communicate what you feel by using your voice. "I" statements are a great place to start.

"I" statements have everything to do with communicating with others. According to goodtherapy.org, "Couples often get trapped in a potentially vicious cycle of perpetual blame without ever addressing the underlying feelings or attachment issues that may be leading to conflict." When you're in conflict, and you're ready to tell somebody how you're feeling, stick with "I" statements.

It may be tempting to say something like, "Stop acting like a dumbass and get your shit together." And hey, maybe you've already tried that avenue of communication. But you're here reading this. So, clearly how you were communicating in the past wasn't working.

Ultimately, you don't have the authority to tell somebody that they are to blame for how you feel. I know it sounds fucking strange but no matter how much that person has wronged you, at the end of the day you are responsible for your feelings. That makes you a badass.

Doesn't that feel damn good?

Finding Your Damn Voice

The formula for finding your damn voice is easier than simple math. I promise because I still use my fingers to count on. Hey, just being honest here!

Here's a simple formula I use in my practice from goodtherapy.org that shows how to use your voice effectively: I feel ____ because ___ when ____. What I need is _____.

Let's break the Using Your Voice Formula down into manageable bites:

Step 1: I feel ____

Example: I feel <u>frustrated</u>

Step 2: Because _____

Example: I feel <u>frustrated</u> because <u>I waited three hours for you to call</u>

Step 3: When _____

Example: I feel <u>frustrated</u> because <u>I waited three hours for you to call </u>when <u>we agreed to talk at a specific time. </u>

Step 4: What I need is _____

Example: I feel <u>frustrated</u> because <u>I waited three hours for you to call </u>when <u>we agreed to talk at a specific time. </u>What I need is <u>for our calls to happen at the time we agreed.</u>

Take full ownership and responsibility for your part. Keep in mind it doesn't excuse any inappropriate or unacceptable behavior from another person. You're just stating that you've got feelings, you've got needs, and you want to voice it for your benefit.

Tiana's Truth

Tiana is someone who hates confrontation. She'd rather run a marathon in heels before confronting her truth. She used to let people walk all over her and hold in how she truly was feeling. Together we began creating her boundaries. Discovering self-love and her self-worth helped her gain a clear idea of what she wanted and didn't want in her relationship.

It finally hit her, this entire time she had been letting her Micah call the shots. And quite literally because his drinking bothered the hell out of her. On the flip side, she felt confused. Micah was a loving, fantastic guy when he was sober, but then they would go out to a party and drink with friends, he would say nasty things to her.

She didn't want to leave the relationship because, in spite of the drinking, he was a nice person. He had a great job, was driven, financially stable, yet he acted like a crazy person when he drank.

Tension and arguments escalated as she grew frustrated with the cycle. When she told him how embarrassed she was when he was drunk, Micah argued that maybe he drank too much because of her. Besides, it was just who he was and was not a problem. For a while, he pulled back from drinking, and she felt like their relationship was changing for the better, and then he'd go back all in.

I asked her how it would look to speak her truth and have a conversation with him about it. Difficult conversations with your partner give you the courage and strength to find your boundaries in a relationship.

What Tiana wanted to tell him was that if he didn't stop drinking, she wasn't sure if she could continue the relationship. But she was scared and worried about the outcome. She loved him so much.

I asked Tiana, "What would you need to make sure you are honoring your self-worth, self-love, and boundaries?" She took a deep breath, sighed, and stated, "I need to talk to him because I am not sure I can continue being in a relationship with someone like this."

From there, Tiana was given the green light to speak her truth and feelings. She acknowledged how she felt and expressed it with her partner. From that point on, it didn't matter how he responded. Well, it did, but she knew she'd be ok no matter what he did. This also opened the dialogue for them to figure out what does and doesn't work for them. I suggested Tiana say, "I feel uncomfortable when you drink too much, and I am figuring out if I truly want to continue being together."

It's Up to You

The thing is, it's up to you to figure out what it is you

want. You can't control the other person. As much as you want to pull out a voodoo doll and start poking pins in, it's just not going to work.

Others may be taken back when you speak your truth. You've played this small role for so long that you no longer need to hold onto it. Your words are your authentic self. Without them, you will continue living in fear and for another person. You've always had this ability to speak up. Now you've got the courage to move forward because hey, self-care.

 Damn Good Affirmation: #MyVoiceIsPowerful

 Create a mantra that will empower you to use your voice.

USE THAT VOICE TO CREATE A BOMB-ASS LIFE

The phrase, *all you need is a balanced life,* sometimes feels like a cheesy ass blanket phrase that should be on an annoying social media advertisement. Feeling stressed? Ah, you need balance. Feeling tired? Ah-ha, balance. Feeling like a failure at love? Balance is the cure. *All you need is balance!*

Have you ever not had your shit together but tried to prove to the outside world you did? Most likely, you put on your fake ass smile, raised your voice a couple of octaves higher and repeatedly nodded saying, "It's fine, my life is great." Meanwhile, your relationship was burning up in uncontrollable flames in the background. How do you fix it? Balance! Yes, I'm kidding.

The only way to successfully achieve balance is to take care of your damn self. Self-care is essential when keeping the fire going in a healthy love life. It all starts with you. Yes, it takes two to be in a healthy relationship, but if you don't set the standard for yourself, you're going to be—let's just say—nodding with a fake smile while the flames burn up behind you.

Self-Care and Chicken Wings

Your self-care sets the standard for breaking free

from codependent relationships. The relationship with your-self is the foundation for all other relationships. Investing in your self-care is essentially priceless. And literally, it can be. You don't need to go to a fancy spa and get a massage. Although that's nice, there are subtle and easy ways that cost nothing to practice.

Think of self-care like your new BFF. It's that friend that's always down to compliment you and make you feel better. And the best part, she's there whenever you need her. But before you jump right into exchanging texts with your new "self-care" BFF, let's take pause.

To access self-care, you need to be honest about your love life. You can't have a healthy love life without self-care, AKA you can't devour buffalo wings without the hot sauce (sorry vegans).

Your awareness is the thought of eating the wings. The action is your hand grabbing the wing and sticking that bad boy in your mouth. Practicing self-care is feeding the hunger. It's part of our basic needs, yet we can get distract-ed by our hunger pains. Sometimes we get used to being in survival mode and do just what we do to get by.

Choose to put yourself and care before survival. Notice the chicken wings sitting in front of you. Pause and make a conscious choice. Do you want to take your first bite or not?

Previously, I would never pick up the hot wings. Instead, I sat in the burning hot sauce thinking about how to make my boyfriend at the time happy and make our relationship work. My biggest fear was that it wouldn't work. So, I'd put everything I had into the relationship. It was like

94

turning onto a dead-end street expecting to find a short cut.

You see, I never put the focus on me and my needs. Instead, I wanted to prove to this guy that I was worthy of being loved by him. I was missing the point. What I needed to prove was I could take care of myself. With the lack of boundaries came the lack of self-care.

Lack of Boundaries or Self-Care?

Which came first—the lack of self-care or boundaries? I'd say self-care. I could list out all the things I did to neglect my self-care. Ultimately, I didn't love myself. I didn't take care of the need to feel worthy. As a result, I chose a partner who absolutely reflected how crappy I felt on the inside.

You can get all the messages and go on all the vacations you want, but if you don't address the real shit going on, then you're going to be searching for the answers in others who can't give it to you.

Rita was all over the place. She had clinical depression and worked with her therapist to get that under control while also working with me. Simultaneous therapy and coaching are both great tools to cope with codependency.

In our first session, she said she wanted to "save" her relationship. When I asked her what she meant by "save," she explained she'd done everything to make this relationship work out, and nothing was helping. I asked about her finances, hobbies, and career. She begrudgingly responded, "It's horrible, I am in debt. I don't do anything fun for myself, and I hate my job."

I wasn't shocked by her response because when you don't practice self-care, you lose a sense of yourself. I told her, "It's time to get a life." What she needed to do was put herself first. When you're so focused on everyone else, your life becomes a cluster fuck in so many areas.

Show Me the Money

Finances are a huge part of self-care. We don't discuss them much when it comes to relationships. Finances are the number one reason for divorce. You need to cover basic needs such as rent, paying bills, and credit cards. Why is this so important to codependents? When you don't have financial boundaries, you may lean on someone to help you with yours, or you might be the one taking care of someone else. It goes both ways.

Sometimes people have the illusion they can't leave unhealthy relationships because of their finances. Maybe their partner is controlling their finances, or they feel trapped because they don't have any money. When you take care of your finances, you have a better chance of choosing the life you want. Money doesn't buy you happiness, but it sure as hell buys you freedom.

You need to figure out what you truly need. Don't know where to start? These four steps will help give you the bomb-ass life you've always wanted. Let's get started.

Four Steps to a Bomb-Ass Life

Step 1 - Ask for help.

Asking for help is one of the biggest obstacles of true self-care. Sometimes when you neglect yourself so much, asking for help feels shameful. It's time to put the survival mentality aside and create a life of fulfillment. Whether it's finances, health, hobbies, spirituality, or love; it's time to get a fucking life! You no longer have to be a prisoner of yourself. You get to choose a pretty fucking awesome life.

Seeds wait to germinate until three needs are met: water, correct temperature (warmth), and a good location (such as in soil). During its early stages of growth, the seedling relies upon the food supplies stored with it in the seed until it is large enough for its leaves to begin making food through photosynthesis.

Your life is like a seed that is yearning to become a strong as fuck tree. Ultimately, you need to nourish the seed with water, find the right temperature, and locate a good place to grow (like soil) for the seed to sprout into a seedling. You are that all-important seed. As you grow into a tree, consider each branch to be a different aspect of your life, including finances, spirituality, love, career, and hobbies. When you forget to water the tree, it either dies or goes into a serious state of dehydration.

When you only focus on sprinkling water on the branches, but ignore watering the seed (roots of your tree), then you end up with some neglected tree branches. The entire tree won't survive because you aren't focusing on what really matters (you, duh!). You need a sturdy tree trunk to keep you balanced and thriving. Often, it's easy to focus on only one aspect of your life (like the career tree branch) because you feel you have the most control in that area of your life. When you focus only on your love life, all the branches of your tree suffers. Eventually, because you aren't watering or nourishing your tree properly, you neglect important areas of your life, and you hold yourself back from experiencing your colorful bloom.

The beautiful thing about growing from a seedling into a full-blown tree is that you get to grow and bloom when the timing is right. You don't get to decide what happens to you, but you do get to choose how you want to grow from it. You're the seed. And the more you nurture yourself with self-care, the more you thrive.

Step 2 - Recognize what is stopping you.

This is key. Awareness has got to be here, girl. Sometimes we're so "in it" that we don't see what has been holding us up. Brooke said she felt selfish putting herself first. She kept hearing her mom and grandmother's voice stating she shouldn't be so self-centered.

The truth is, it's selfish not to take care of yourself. By doing so, you'll never find a healthy partner. The questions are, "What is causing you not to focus on yourself? What's that same old shit you're telling yourself repeatedly that's preventing you from showing up for yourself?" Whatever it is, that's what you need to do when it comes to self-care. Nobody is perfect. To keep on track, know what your triggers are.

In the past, I thought if I left my partner, he would no longer like me. The truth is, it doesn't matter what their reaction is. You want to be with a partner who loves and values the crap out of you because you take care of yourself. And if they don't, run.

Step 3 - Create your dream life.

Girl, dream big or go the hell home. Seriously. Enough playing it small and quiet. What do you want for your life?

Rita had no clue what she wanted except that she was 110 percent certain she wanted her relationship to work. Despite a major "in flight" malfunction that was getting in the way of her relationship succeeding, she wanted it to work.

If you are focused on the outcome and don't pay attention to other areas of your life, such as hobbies, career, finances—watch out! Don't be surprised if you don't get the outcome you want. Focus on the journey. You can't get to the outcome you want unless you take the journey.

Find things that genuinely interest you and that you enjoy. This is your chance to really start to build yourself up and find joy in things that aren't stressful. Be in the company of whatever it is you enjoy.

Courageous Action Warrior Activity:

To get started, write a list under each of the five

categories. For example, under hobbies, you might write photography, brunch with girlfriends, listening to podcasts, and yoga.

Now, select one from each of the five categories that really speak to you. For example, you may choose yoga from your hobby list.

Now it's time to put one foot in front of the other and do the damn thing.

Step 4 - Get moving!

It's easy to have your thoughts on paper, but it's quite another to live it. It can be terrifying to move your awareness aside and focus on action instead. Don't worry; I have my clients participate in this Courageous Action Warrior Activity where they essentially create the want, game plan the action, and take that sucker home.

Courageous Action Warrior Activity:

It's time to get creative and make your move. Have fun with this! Which hobby or activity do you want to pursue in the area of your finances, hobbies, spirituality, health, or love? Create a realistic day to day schedule and mark out days or times that you can fit your activity in. This could be as simple as looking up yoga classes online that work around your schedule. From there, pick the date, class and time, and then follow through on it.

Disclaimer: Don't be surprised if taking action increases the way you feel about yourself. It may have been a long time since you've done something just for you. And a bonus: allow yourself to enjoy it. Chances are, feelings of guilt or discomfort will show up at first. That's fine. Reflect on why this could be coming up.

Get a Life

Real talk, sister. This isn't a quick fix to happiness, but it sure as hell is what gives you your life back. The more you practice self-care, the more it contributes to a successful relationship. Patience is your best friend. Creating your best life won't happen overnight. If anything, this becomes a journey of growth and compassion.

No matter what your relationship status is, when you get a life, you won't be dependent on your partner to make you happy and fulfilled. You'll have everything you need to nourish that shit out of your seed. Your partner will just become that extra guacamole from Chipotle, making your life a bit more colorful.

You've got everything you need at your fingertips. Now, it's time to pull out your wand and make shit happen. Don't worry; I'd never throw you into something without a plan on how to be successful at it. That's why in the next chapter, I'll share my process for taking control of your damn life.

 Damn Good Affirmation: #IAmSelfCare

 How is self-care beneficial in your life?

MAKE IT HAPPEN, GIRL IT'S TIME!

Now is the time to take control of *your* life instead of taking control of everybody else's lives. When you stop putting the focus on someone else, it is like jump-starting your phone battery that's needed to be full for quite some time.

It's easy to see what's wrong with the other person. They need to:

- Take care of themselves.
- Show how they care about you.
- Pay attention to your needs.

But guess what? You're the only one who can set the standard on how you are treated. This doesn't mean you need to excuse their behavior, but it's time to put some pep in your damn step, girl!

You'll legit go blue in the face if you try and make the other person see how amazing you are. Trust me, I've experienced this, and it wasn't because I could eat an entire carton of Michigan blueberries in one sitting! You must create your own amazing and put that into action.

Tons of people are aware of their situation and do nothing about it. You aren't one of those people. You're someone who knows it's time to step into your worth. You don't need to do it perfectly to see a positive change in your intimate relationships.

There's this misconception that everyone has got "life down." Well, news flash, they don't. They aren't even coming close. No one has it figured out, but there is depth to showing up for your own happiness. In a codependent mindset, you're constantly replaying scenarios in your mind and having conversations with people that aren't in the room. The real change is to shift the obsessions of others to your own needs.

Expect the Best, Prepare for the Worst

Outcomes are a funny thing. We often prepare ourselves so much for the worse, and it rarely happens. Waiting for the next shoe to drop is exhausting. It's like you're prepping for the ultimate battle when you're really headed to the beach to watch the sunset.

Up to this point, your illusion of control has helped you cope with all this chaos. It's allowed you to feel like you've had your shit together even when your house was already burnt and smoking. Meanwhile, the jokes on you. You're still standing there waiting for the flame with your hose. It's time to move forward. Don't let the illusion of control hold you hostage to the beautiful life and relationship you're damned capable of having. You're too worthy for that crap. If you decide to stay down there, then it's a conscious choice you're making. You get to choose how you want to live your life.

If you want to:

- Change your relationship, it's time to do it now.
- Break up, it's time to do it now.
- Date, it's time to do it now.
- Take ownership of your life and create amazing relationships, it's time to do it now.

There is never a right time and place to make these decisions. If you wait for the "right time and place" you'll be waiting forever. There is no waiting around for someone to call the shots for you. You were not meant to spend your entire life in codependent relationships. You deserve amazing, loving, healthy relationships.

It is time to take full control over your life. When it comes down to making real tangible changes, you've got to be your own cheerleader. Take these six steps to get back control of your life.

Take Control of Your Life

Step 1 - Look in the mirror

Step 2 - Release control with spirituality

Step 3 - Reshape how you think about yourself

Step 4 - Take care of yourself

Step 5 - Set boundaries

Step 6 - Ask for help

Step 1 - Look in the mirror

Change starts by recognizing you play a part in every relationship issue you have. It doesn't matter how much you feel fucked over by this person, figure out what part you are playing.

Ask yourself: How have you contributed to codependency in this relationship?

Ashley always made excuses for her boyfriend Gordon's unacceptable behavior. She would clean up after him and miss girl's nights with her friends because he wasn't taking care of himself. Ashley recognized she was afraid that if she didn't help him, it would mean she didn't love him.

Eventually, Ashley discovered she was enabling Gordon instead of giving love. She now knew she needed to take responsibility for her part in the relationship by finding a new way to redefine and create love in their relationship.

Ask yourself: What are your motives?

For Ashley, her motives for taking care of Gordon were she didn't want the relationship to fall apart, she loved the recognition she got for how much she'd done for him, and she didn't want others to think there was something wrong in their relationship. She wanted to appear in control of the relationship, while in reality, she felt totally out of control.

Step 2 - Release control with spirituality

I'm not going to bullshit you here. Giving up control is so much easier said than done. When you're in a codependent relationship, naturally, you default to trying to control the other person, situations, or outcomes. Why? Because life feels so damn hectic and out of control.

When you've got limited or absolutely zero boundaries or self-care in place, then you see the relationship as one. Their actions are a direct result of your behavior or their actions threaten how you feel and function throughout the day. The good news is you don't have to do it alone when you've got spirituality.

There's a difference between spirituality and religion. My girl Merriam over at Merriam-Webster states that religion is, "a personal set or institutionalized system of religious attitudes, beliefs, and practices." Maybe you've experienced being baptized, fasting for Ramadan, or partying to some good tunes to celebrate your bat mitzvah.

Think of spirituality as something that's not an organized institution, but allows you to incorporate it into your life. According to author Phillip Sheldrake in his book, *A Brief History of Spirituality,* "Spirituality tends to focus either on individual self-realization or on some kind of inwardness. There is considerable justification for this assertion in consumerist 'lifestyle spirituality' that promotes fitness, healthy living, and holistic well-being." So, yes, if you've ever participated in SoulCycle, reiki, yoga, or shopped for crystals, then you've been a consumer of spirituality.

Here's the deal with spirituality: there are no rules. You can make it whatever you want. Your Higher Power can be your gut, intuition, or even your house plant because you know something greater out there created it. It's not always about religion. Atheists can be spiritual too. The only proof you need is that you can't control the waves in an ocean or whether it's going to rain on your wedding day. Something else controls that, and it's not you.

If you struggle with spirituality, you are not alone. It's totally normal. I've been there and completely resisted it before. And guess what? Today I am a spiritual person. My gut and intuition define my Higher Power. Embracing it has helped me find healthy partners and be in healthy relationships. Without my Higher Power, I'd be lost in relationships. Now I know that I've never been alone and can only do so much before allowing my Higher Power to take over.

Ask yourself: Do you remember a shitty time in your life where you thought you couldn't get through it?* And then somehow *you* did. That might be spirituality.

I was not a spiritual person for the longest time. I *knew* there was something greater than myself—a Higher Power—but I had a pretty fucking hard time releasing control. Let's just say I was an inner control freak. Once I found my spirituality, it was a serious game-changer in my relationships. Whatever my relationship status, I was able to find happiness regardless of the pain. I'm not BSing you either.

My mind stopped spinning in circles with fear and anxiety of what someone else was doing or not doing and how I was going to be ok in the situation.

It's not to say that I *didn't* feel anger, sadness, or happiness. I'm human, so yeah, I felt all of that. But with spirituality, I knew I could get through any love obstacle with a new way to *trust* that it would all work out. Somehow in between the thoughts of, "Am I ever going to get through this?" and "Holy shit I got through it." Something made it happen. That *something* is what I call spirituality.

I was facilitating a workshop, and I asked the participants to write down how they release control with spirituality. Abby raised her hand and said she struggled with this as that part of her identity felt she needed to take care of others.

I asked Abby to think about the things in life that were "coincidences." She listed off a few which included getting her dream job by meeting the recruiter at a friend's birthday party. In reality, she didn't have any control over that happening. All she could control over was showing up for the interview, getting her resume together, and negotiating her contract.

At what point during the interview process, did she think, "I have full control over the final decision?" Never. That was nerve-wracking for her. I asked her to think about a time when everything worked out when she didn't think it would. It happened when she was with her boyfriend who cheated on her. At the time, she felt so lost and confused. She didn't see how she would be able to go on, but here she was four years later and was not with this person anymore. She was still alive. When I asked about what it would be like to not worry about controlling the outcome or results, she responded, "Serene."

I explained she only has to show up for her part. Life is a matter of releasing the need for a result. Although Abby didn't get what she wanted, it was ok. Sometimes we can't see where we are headed but knowing something greater than us is taking care of the unknown provides us with a sense of release. We no longer feel the need to control the outcome or others.

Abby shared, "I suppose letting go of the idea that I have control over my outcomes helps me see there is something out there bigger than myself. This force continues moving me in the direction I am supposed to be in. This helps me let go of control and allow what is."

You can hand your worries or fears over to a spiritual source and know that you're not in control of the outcome of the choices you make with another person. You're not in control of what's going to happen in any situation with someone else. That's up to your spiritual source.

All you can do is focus on putting one foot in front of the other and trust that when you do your part, you're allowing things to come into your life on life's terms. It's not a hidden agenda of what you want at that moment.

Ask yourself: When was a time you gave up control and thought something didn't work out, but surprisingly, it worked itself out?

Step 3 - Reshape how you think about yourself

At times, codependency makes us feel like ultimate failures when we can't fix the situation or the person we love. But, keep in mind, it's not who you are but what you allow to feel and become real. It's like banging your head against the wall expecting the pain to stop. The only thing that will stop the pain is to stop creating it in the first place.

Shelby was fed the hell up with her boyfriend, Stephen. She tried pouring out his bottles of alcohol to convince herself he wasn't driving drunk. During our session, she had a breakthrough—he had nothing she wanted, and she no longer wanted to be with him.

I asked her what the relationship was giving her. She replied, "Nothing." She knew she wanted to end things for good. But Shelby continued to hold on because she didn't want to be alone. She eventually recognized she felt more alone with Stephen than without him.

That was an ah-ha moment for her. She kept being pulled back in through his false promises to change. She finally had enough. In her gut, she knew it was over, but she felt she wasn't deserving of finding someone else, and she didn't want to start over again. Why? Because she wasn't ready to face the truth.

Over time she worked on affirmations. Shelby's "go to" was, "I am not enough." Together we worked on flipping it around to, "I am worthy." This helped her change her negative thinking to positive. But that wasn't enough. She needed to begin making choices that allowed her to show up for herself. And this is what I call self-care.

Step 4 - Take care of yourself

There is nothing more powerful than to respect yourself so much that you take responsibility for your own care.

I'll be 100 percent honest. Early on, I did not understand self-care. I felt that doing something for myself was selfish and wrong because I wasn't putting someone else first. So, what did I do? Over and over again, I abandoned my needs. Eventually, I couldn't take it any longer. So, I learned how to implement self-care. After I went through my self-growth and self-love journey, I began dating Robert. We dated for about a year and a half.

Toward the end of our relationship, I felt him pulling away. I could feel he wasn't as into me anymore. What I did was different than anything I'd ever done before in a relationship. Instead of ignoring my needs and catering to him, I took the contrary action. I practiced self-care.

I started to act on the things that I needed for me. I made sure I was going to the gym and staying on top of healthy eating. I was putting myself first. Was I still showing up for my boyfriend at the time? Yes. In previous relationships, when things were off like sour milk, I'd drop everything and cling to pleasing them. As I learned to practice self-care, I recognized that shit ain't cute no more.

He eventually broke up with me. It's true—we had a healthy non-codependent relationship, and he still broke up with me. Guess what? I was totally ok! I moved out of our apartment the next weekend. I continued my routine even though I felt sad and was grieving a breakup. I was able to move on because I was taking care of my finances, health, and fitness.

This is all about self-care.

Ask yourself:
- *What is it you need to do today to show up for yourself?*
- *What would it look like if you practiced self-care?*
- *What has stopped you from practicing self-care?*
- *How will you practice self-care this week?*

Step 5 - Set boundaries

Boundaries? Yeah, about these. I figured it was healthy if I bent over backward for the guy I was madly in love with. Well, I can officially tell you it isn't healthy. If you decide to jump into someone else's hula hoop that shit's going to stop spinning, so yeah, stay in your own hula hoop.

Tessie became friends with Pat, who she met in her boxing class. Tessie's last serious relationship was toxic as her ex lied and cheated multiple times. She had been single for about a year and was recently dating. As she puts it, she wasn't going to compromise anything again for a dude.

Pat was married and separated from his wife for the past two years although they decided to give it another go. He would text Tessie and compliment her, a lot. She was flattered and felt a sexual attraction to Pat but knew he was off-limits. She questioned whether his wife cared that they spent so much time texting. Instead of playing into the attention, which felt good, she knew she needed to set a boundary out of respect for herself. She texted Pat and let him know that she appreciated their friendship, but felt a bit uncomfortable now that he and his wife were living together. She asked him to stop texting so many compliments to her.

Tessie wasn't going to compromise her worth and respect for someone who couldn't match it. Fast forward six months later. Pat informed her he and his wife were officially getting a divorce. In a roundabout way, he implied he wanted to date her. Was she excited? Yeah, because she felt the same intimate feelings. However, for him to be considered dateable, he needed to hit a few requirements.

For Tessie, these requirements include:

- Being emotionally available, meaning he was no longer living with his ex-wife.
- Taking appropriate measures to begin the divorce process.
- Being willing to continue to grow through therapy or other professional help.

She soon recognized they were not in the same place emotionally. As a result, she decided not to jump in headfirst with Pat. She took it slow. She chose to create boundaries to make sure the work she had done to break free of codependency was being carried out with Pat.

She did this because it was not worth getting into

another codependent relationship. She'd been there and swam through relationships like this before. This time she didn't want to go back into the deep end. Tessie wanted to be with someone who reflected the self-care, positive thinking, spirituality, and ownership that she had for herself.

Ask yourself:
- *What are the requirements you have for someone you are in a relationship with?*
- *How will you implement boundaries into your intimate relationships?*

Step 6 - Ask for help

You don't have to go through codependency alone. Even though it feels isolating at times and you may feel you're the only one who is experiencing it, ya ain't.

There are a ton of resources out there that can help you say goodbye to codependency for good, including finding:

- A therapist to deal with any childhood issue or trauma.
- A dating and relationship coach who specializes in this area.
- Twelve-step programs such as Al-Anon, Codependents Anonymous, Adult Children of Alcoholics, or Sex and Love Addicts Anonymous

Keep in mind every therapist, coach, program, and meeting have their own vibe and personality. If one doesn't work for you, try others. You can only receive help when you're ready. You decide when the time is right for you.

Break Free

So, you're ready to break the hell free from codependency. You've got the tools and tricks up your Topshop sleeve, and now it's time to make lasting change. You know, for damn good. To get the results you want, you'll need accountability. In the next chapter, you'll learn how to make accountability your new BFF.

 Damn Good Affirmation: #LetGoLetGod

 After reviewing these six steps, how do you most want to take control of your life? Why?

CHAPTER 10

BREAK FREE FROM CODEPENDENCY FOR DAMN GOOD

You can't get shit done without taking action, and you can't take action without being accountable. According to the Merriam Webster dictionary, the definition of accountability is the quality or state of being accountable, *especially*: an obligation or willingness to accept responsibility or to account for one's actions.

Sometimes wanting to make changes in your love life can leave you feeling like you're running up a mountain that's steep as hell. You run out of oxygen 'cause let's get real; there's elevation. Then you feel like a failure as you're standing there gasping for breath still looking up at the top of the mountain.

The Secret to….

We live in a society where it's all about results. And we don't want typical results. That's why we fall for those get rich quick schemes offering the most promising results. Many ads on Facebook or other social media platforms are about finding the secret to weight loss, love, body fat, aging, sex, and so much more. If all these people knew all these secrets, why are we still looking for solutions?

But I do have some wisdom bombs to drop on ya.

The secret to getting shit done is *you.* No one is going to hold your hand or pull you out of a crowd and show you the way. You've got to hold your own damn hand. Stay aligned and determined to make changes in your love life. As you become more accountable to yourself, your results become your superpower to growth.

By being accountable, you get to explore and truly embrace your authentic self. Just remember, the only thing that stands between you and making successful changes in your relationship is *you.*

Don't play the comparison game by measuring your growth. No matter how much someone else's life looks put together on social media doesn't mean it's true. When you begin to compare your love life to others because they seem to be happy, keep in mind, they're probably doing the same as well.

When I was ready to break up with Jake, I sent a group text to my family. I told them I was headed over to Jake's to break up with him. When I tried to break up with him before, he'd always somehow turn the conversation around to giving him one more "chance."

I'm glad I group texted my intention because when I tried to break up with him, he started gaslighting me. He told me I was not in the right or healthy mindset. As a result, I didn't break up with him until the next day only because I let my mom and two sisters in on what was happening. I couldn't hide away my reality. Calling my therapist the following day was the Sherlock Holmes evidence of my accountability.

Disclaimer: When my anxiety starts coming back, I reach out to my therapist. FYI, going to therapy is another form of accountability. When I find myself in this place, I pray to my Higher Power to remove anxiety on their time. With a therapist's assistance, I'm able to move along much more quickly.

I digress. That evening was a total God shot moment where I knew my Higher Power was looking out for me. Even when you think things aren't working out the way you planned, be patient, it will happen. No matter what you try to do that doesn't work out, the right choice will be made for you regardless of who tries to get in the way of it.

The truth is, Jake did me a favor by gaslighting me that evening. It's one of those moments I can look back and say, "Jokes on you." He questioned my psychological state, and as a result, I reached out to my therapist for help. I thought I was the crazy one. I wasn't, though. I was just a 24-year-old young woman who lacked self-love and self-worth. In turn, I was in an intimate relationship with Jake, who was emotionally unavailable. Without being account-able to my family, I wouldn't have ended it or stood up for myself.

Are you ready to hold yourself accountable?

To hold yourself accountable, start by setting a dead-line. Once you figure out what it is you need or want to do, make it real by scheduling that deadline.

Now if you're someone who feels pressure when you think about getting shit done by a certain date, listen up. I am calling total BS on the idea that time heals everything. You can let time pass by as long as you want. If you don't create a way to grow through that time, then you're going to be where you started one year, five years or 20 years down the line. You are your own healer. Time is just another thing you can add to your accountability toolbox.

My clients use deadlines for all types of things. I've had clients select dates for ending a relationship. I've had clients use a time frame for when they were going to have a conversation with the person they were interested in pursuing. I have also had clients use dates to check in with themselves, so checking in becomes routine. This helps gauge whether they're staying on top of what they need.

At a recent workshop, I shared that making New Year New Me goals was total BS. You don't need a new *you*. *You're* the foundation for making changes. If you can commit to a time frame, then it becomes much more manageable.

After the workshop, Kelley shared that she felt too overwhelmed and panicked to commit to a certain day to get back in the dating world. I suggested looking at it as one day at a time. Instead of focusing on dating, I encouraged her to look at what she needs to do to "get back out there." For her, that meant breaking this into bite-sized pieces, also known as growth.

Be honest with yourself: You will never make progress if you aren't telling the truth about your lack of accountability.

When Lauren and I first started working together,

she was worried she would fall back into the same trap with her ex. In the past, he would reach out, and she'd feel obligated to respond and eventually go back to him. Lauren managed to break up with him.

During our third session, Lauren blurted out she talked to her ex after the breakup. She said she thought about lying to me, but if she did, then she wasn't committing to change. Lauren felt like a failure for picking up the phone when he called. We all know we can be our own worst critic.

I asked her what she learned from their conversation. She was surprised that I wasn't contributing to her self-hatred narrative. She shared how she grew as a result of the conversation. It felt like a significant turning point. Lauren had never been honest with anyone before cutting off communication with her ex. If she failed, she was afraid everyone would see her as weak because she couldn't commit to something. I said to her, "We can only fail if we do nothing. But we can only grow if we do it imperfectly. Honesty is the catalyst for change."

Keep in mind, if someone lies to you, it's not about you. If someone can't tell you the truth, they've yet to practice being truthful with themselves. Honesty starts within.

Trust yourself: When creating a new relationship, you slowly build trust with your partner as you gain confidence that they will be there for you. A great way to practice building healthy trust in relationships is by starting with *yourself*, girl. You need to be accountable to yourself.

I was working with Georgina for about five months before she was ready to confidently get back into the dating world after ending things with her boyfriend who was addicted to pain meds. She was nervous about getting back out there. I lie, she was terrified because she felt she couldn't trust herself to pick the right guy. She knew she would be devastated if she got into another relationship with someone who had deep-rooted issues like her ex. I told her, "I get that. It's normal to feel that way because you went through a lot of shit."

I asked her if she felt she was in the same place emotionally as she was five months ago. She replied, "No, it's because I've taken action to make changes like working with you, and it's allowed me to grow."

From there, I pointed out how resourceful she is. When things feel off, she takes action. Georgina instantly felt relief recognizing that part of building trust within was looking at how she already handles situations.

Create a schedule: Blocking out time in your daily routine is gold. Using resources to help you get there like a planner or Google calendar can work like magic.

Codependency looks the same in the LGBTQ community. I started working with Paige, who was about one year into her marriage. At this point, she discovered she was only living for her wife Dini's happiness. This created tension in the marriage. Paige was unable to take care of herself, and as a result, she struggled with communication. Ultimately, this made Dini feel as if she couldn't talk with her.

Paige had lost the sense of who she was. She felt helpless and ashamed but knew she needed to kick her life back into gear if she wanted to save her marriage. During our first session, Paige confessed she didn't do anything for herself that brought her joy.

When she shared her daily routine, it was apparent she was scheduling her activities to fit the needs of her wife. I asked her to share something she wanted to try doing even if she felt intimidated. She immediately responded, "Dancing." Tears welled in her eyes as she said, "Dancing used to be my self-expression. It's who I am. I haven't danced in four years."

Together we came up with a personalized and curated day-to-day schedule for her to try. When we met again, Paige was excited to share she felt grounded for the first time in who knows how long. Creating a weekly schedule was the catalyst for getting her damn life back. It all goes back to being accountable to yourself.

Finding Your Hype Squad

The people you hold near and dear are the people you want to be in your Hype Squad. These are the people who love you for *you.* And hey, maybe your Hype Squad is just one person, or maybe it's your dog. It doesn't matter. It's the force that gives you a genuine connection and hopes for tomorrow.

Your Hype Squad looks out for your best interest and are there to catch you after a shit relationship or break up. When you find these people, hang onto them. You'll need them when times get tough.

It's hard to make changes alone (I highly recommend not doing this alone). Consider your Hype Squad to be your support system. If you don't have a Hype Squad, go out and find one. Belonging and connection keep you alive and thriving no matter what happens in your relationships.

Coping with Codependency Daze

I'm going to get super real with you. I wish someone told me this when I was going through my codependency daze. I felt alone. I didn't know where or who to turn to. I overshared with co-workers and made my anxiety and future-tripping my Higher Power.

Recognize the truth. You're not alone. You were never alone. No matter how isolating it feels when you're wracked with shame and fear, you are not by yourself. You belong. You always have. You always will.

No matter how much pain a person has put you through, it doesn't define who you are. It doesn't dictate your fate with future relationships. After being trapped in multiple codependent relationships, I thought I'd never find the right person. But, it was never about finding the right person. It was about my growth.

I may have lost sight of shore many times as I searched deep within my bones for who I was. Each time my Hype Squad brought me back to myself. No matter how much I hated myself, my Hype Squad showed me how lovable and capable I was of making changes. While I didn't rely on my Hype Squad for validation, they gave me nuggets of hope and reflection. With their positive reinforcement, I recognized I was capable of growth and change.

I decided to get to work. I pulled out my shovel and dug deep. I planted and nourished the seed of hope not by just watering my seed, but paying attention to how often and what time of day it needed watering.

Time for Some Action

Do planning and taking action make you feel uncomfortable? Hell yeah. Is it normal to question yourself as you go through it? Absolutely. Will you want to back out? Yep. These are normal feelings. By being accountable, you can make these feelings step aside.

You've got to figure this out, realize where you're off and learn how to be on point. Keep in mind, overthinking kills happiness. Don't do so much work that you burn out and don't think so hard you talk yourself out of change. The idea is to have positive thoughts so that your actions reflect your inner talk AKA telling your Inner Peggy to pipe down.

 Damn Good Affirmation: #IveGotThis

 What one thing do you want to hold yourself accountable to? How will you do that?

SWAP-SPIT WITH POSITIVITY

If this girl, who grew up with domestic violence, was in multiple codependent relationships and can peace out on codependency for damn good, then so can you, girlfriend! Here's the truth though. I'm not magical. I'm not anything extraordinary with mythical powers. I'm just someone who got tired of living shit relationship after shit relationship with no self-love.

I unleashed my confident warrior by stepping into my damn worth. I made lemonade out of the lemons and dumped in a crap ton of sugar. Why? Because I am worth it.

Is This My Ticket?

Now, breaking free of codependency for damn good isn't a guaranteed ticket to happiness. You're going to have to make a mental effort at creating these changes. It's a mindset. Like her or not, Taylor Swift didn't become the youngest artist to win a Grammy or have the highest-grossing North America tour by thinking she couldn't do it.

Instead, she strategized, took risks, and continued to push through, even when her reputation went to shit when Kim Kardashian leaked a video recording of Kanye and Taylor. Just Google it. As Taylor says, "I never trust a narcissist, but they love me." Maybe you can relate to that. No matter how much the other person loves you, put the trust back into yourself.

Stop telling yourself that you can't get through this. It's in the darkest moments, the lowest of lows, that you will still have the strength to swim through this thing called life. Just know, feeling damn good is on the other side of your fear, self-sabotage, and doubt.

You've got a choice. Step into your heels and create your own catwalk or continue walking in the sand with your heels not properly strapped to your feet.

Will They Go Away?

Do codependent tendencies pop up even if you put in all this inner badass work? Could be. It's normal. Some of this behavior is the only thing you've ever experienced in your lifetime. It's like a default button. But like my client Marta has noticed, these tendencies pop up from time to time.

After working on her codependent tendencies, Marta was in a healthy, loving relationship and argued with her boyfriend over whose turn it was to wash the dishes. She instantly felt she needed to make the situation better by being responsible for her partner getting frustrated and walking out of the kitchen. Marta wanted to make everything ok. Instead, she paused and reflected on the situation. And guess what? The feelings passed.

Even if you do everything you can (and for shits and gigs add some backflips) being free from codependency is not your ticket to quick fix "happy, happy" relationships

24 damn 7. Why? Because that would still be living in the codependent mindset. You can't rely on having everything be amazing to feel complete.

Following through on these changes will make life and relationships so much damn better. And if you're no longer living in mental prison chaos, then that's fucking awesome!

You're Worth It

Ok, so you may still feel like you're in the Arabian desert with heels, one camel and a free water bottle you got at a mandatory work conference. But, remember you're not alone on this journey. You still might not feel like you have everything you need, but it's time to embrace everything that's happened in your life. There are no mistakes. The only thing that will get you out of the desert is your mindset.

Embrace what is happening for you, which includes every heartbreak, rejection, codependent relationship, and fuck up. It has got you where you are today and made you stronger. There are no mistakes. There are no coincidences. You are exactly where you need to be at this very moment. Every wrong turn was a right turn. Every life confusion had its path.

It's damn time to let that shit go of staying in the past waiting for some person, place, or thing to save you. You are the only one who can save your ass. You've always had it and you always will.

Watch that Inner Peggy (Voice)

Let me introduce you to Inner Peggy, although you've met her before. Maybe you even met her today. Her voice halts you from accomplishing your full potential. Inner Peggy really boils down to self-worth. She's the friend who gives you unsolicited advice and makes you question yourself.

Inner Peggy isn't trying to harm you; she just thinks she knows best. So her unsolicited advice is really just trying to protect you. But, Inner Peggy can rob you from living out your true purpose. As an advocate of fear-based thinking, she allows us to think we aren't good enough.

We all have different reasons for our Inner Peggy, such as trauma, break ups, insults, our upbringing, fear, and so much more. It's different for everyone, but boils down to "you are not good enough." How do you get past it? The answer is sitting in your damn gut. Inner Peggy and your gut are fighting against each other. Somehow, it's easier to listen to Inner Peggy as you've been doing this for so long. Don't tempt your Inner Peggy with a seat at the table.

Sometimes you worry about things that aren't going to happen simply because of that Inner Peggy. These thoughts are just creativity taking up free rent in your mind. Invest in yourself and go after what you want. Focus on taking care of yourself first.

You Get to Choose

Over time it starts to weigh on you; you become stunted at making choices that benefit you in your relationships. You may choose partners who are controlling or manipulative because you do not believe that there will be anyone else who will love you because you may not love yourself. You have a choice in all of this. Chase sunsets, not fear.

When I first started working with Katelyn, she was 33 years old and had been in a three-year codependent relationship. Basically, she didn't want to fuck around with men who were emotionally unavailable as she wanted to get married and start a family. At the time, she had zero trust in herself to find a guy who was right for her. Instead, she relied on the opinions of family members to call the shots of who she was dating. Over time, this only fed into her insecurities.

To heal, she needed to get very specific on who she wanted to be in a relationship with, her boundaries, and then put it to work. So, she did just that. It turned out she knew what she wanted, where she drew the line, and how to trust herself. When a date didn't fit what she wanted, she turned down the next date.

She was looking for the filet mignon, not the In-N-Out burger. The filet mignon understood what it was like to experience growth through aging. Meanwhile, the In-N-Out burger was tasty as hell but came down to a quick fix.

The awesome thing about Katelyn was that she was goal-oriented. She was open and willing to try anything and everything because she so badly didn't want to go back to where she had been.

Within five months of working together, she met Dave. He was kind and had feelings for her but wasn't emotionally available because of a recent breakup. Katelyn expressed to Dave that for them to move forward, they needed to both be in the same place emotionally. In the meantime, Katelyn continued to spend time with Dave. However, she created a boundary for herself that she didn't want to have sex or even kiss Dave. She wanted to be emotionally sober while getting to know him.

Ya know when you just want to get in bed with someone? Well, Katelyn felt the sexual tension building. It made sticking to her boundaries difficult. Katelyn wondered what her timeline should be. How long should she keep playing out this friend thing with Dave? She was feeling anxious and began having Inner Peggy thoughts like if she didn't take action, she might lose a potential relationship with Dave.

As we talked about this, it came down to one simple thing. She needed to stay present to create a foundation for healthy intimacy with Dave. If she made a decision based off needing to move things along too quickly, she would be playing into Inner Peggy.

For the first time, Katelyn recognized she had power over her situation. When I asked Katelyn how she wanted to continue with Dave, she responded, "Continuing my boundaries until I feel comfortable choosing to discuss things with Dave that don't come from Inner Peggy, but what I truly want. I guess I need some time in that space to sit with the discomfort."

Katelyn knew that if she acted on her Inner Peggy by worrying about where her relationship with Dave would go, and acting on that worry, she'd be slipping back into her codependent ways. She recognized she wasn't perfect.

Although her mind may want to lead her back into codependency, she has choices on how to move forward in life.

If I'm honest, at times, I need to remind myself that it's ok to be human. Know that you are not perfect. When you make a mistake, or your thinking takes you to a worry that has yet to happen, remember that you aren't a complete failure. Don't get discouraged. We all make mistakes.

The Silver Lining of Making Mistakes

Stop comparing yourself to others. Relationships take effort, and it starts with you. Nobody's relationship is 100 percent perfect. Everyone is figuring it out as they go. While on social media, be aware of this when comparing your life to others/celebrities.

When you don't get it "right," remind yourself that getting it right doesn't exist. What exists is that things are exactly the way they should be. Show up to life and make choices of what you need for yourself.

After I broke free of my relationship with Jake, I took time off from dating. When I felt ready, I jumped back in armed with new tools. I broke free of codependency. I'm glad I got out of my stinking thinking. Here's the thing, my first non-codependent relationship was with Heath. I felt a little shaky. Could I truly trust myself? Was I going to fuck this up? Would it suddenly be revealed that he was an addict? I didn't let these thoughts stop me from continuing my relationship with him. Over time, things progressed, and we moved in together.

Disclaimer: Let me just say I think living with a person is necessary before marriage. It allows you to find out if you're right for one another.

So, guess what? Our relationship didn't work out. The last three months of living together, I could feel Heath pulling away. We got in a few arguments. I learned that we might be two very different people. I wanted to address that things were feeling off. He said we'd discuss it at another time.

It was a Friday night, and I had just come back from dinner with my friend Selena. (FYI, she somehow is always the person connected to my breakups.) That night we got ice cream in Beverly Hills, and we were driving back to her apartment. She asked if I saw myself ever marrying Heath. I responded, "I could, but there are some communication issues I want to work on together before getting married."

I was driving down Sunset Boulevard on my way home listening to "Something Just Like This" by Coldplay with my hand out the window. The air had a cool warmth, as LA late spring nights tend to be. That's when something spiritual shifted within. My spirit around the relationship lifted as I was having doubts about whether I wanted to be with Heath.

As I walked into the apartment, he said, "I need to talk to you." Instantly my stomach dropped. Like, come on, we all know what that shit means. Yep, he broke up with me. I felt rage, rejection, anger, sadness, abandonment, and relief. As I walked outside to get some air, I looked to the LA sky and felt that calmness from the car ride.

As tears slowly rolled down my cheeks, I took a

deep breath and thanked God. For whatever reason, I was supposed to be standing here on Hacienda Place in this very moment. While I didn't know what tomorrow would bring or what would happen next, I knew deep inside that God's rejection was my protection.

Here's the crazy part. I was ok discovering that non-codependent relationships end too. After all, I had all the tools I needed to get back up on my feet. I had an amazing Hype Team, knew I was in charge of my self-care, and it turns out I'm a mother fuckin' boss with my finances. Breaking up with Heath didn't break me. It made me. I realized no man could take away my self-worth, and no one would ever have power or control over me.

This relationship with Heath was a beautiful lesson. It proved that after years of questionable relationships, I had broken free of codependency. I was capable of a healthy relationship, even if it didn't work out. Nobody can steal my damn crown. The love, worth, and care I have for myself are far too great for anyone to touch.

Focused and confident, I got back into the game when I was ready. I made sure whoever I found would fit into my life and not ask the question, "Did I fit into his life?" I wanted to make sure I found someone to complement my life and wasn't sacrificing myself for someone else.

In love, there are no guarantees. Sometimes relationships are here to provide a lesson. Every ending is a new opportunity for growth. For me, I saw someone who took charge of her life and changed the course of it one moment at a time.

Let's be real. You wouldn't pick up this book if you

didn't think there was a way out of this hell. Breaking free of codependency for damn good simply means you've put yourself first. It starts with you. Now that's my guarantee.

 Damn Good Affirmation: #MyLifeIsAwesome

 In your own words, define what it means for you to break free from codependency.

CONTAGIOUS LOVE ON-LOCK

Contagious love is all about the continuous obses-sion of trying to get your damn relationships "right" only to find yourself confused about why you can't or couldn't get it "right." So, instead, you try going down different avenues and paths to make it work. It keeps following you every-where you go.

Truth be told, so what if you've got codependent ten-dencies or characteristics? The fact that you're here right now means you're taking steps to break free from it all. And that girlfriend, is self-love.

When you accept yourself first, you learn to accept others.

No, I'm not asking you to walk around and do ev-erything by the book, ha! I want you to practice owning the confident warrior within and create that bomb-ass life you deserve. Will you go through times of doubt and wonder what the hell you're doing with your love life? Absolutely. No matter your doubts, the confident warrior strength isn't going anywhere. Even in your darkest moments, you al-ways have it within—even when it feels impossible to reach for—it's there.

Give yourself permission to focus on you. You were built with the strength and resilience to fill your own damn worth with love. You've arrived. Actually, you've landed on the tarmac and have just been sitting there. You now know the steps to become your own hype woman. This is what will guide you while navigating the codependency map. Just remember when you get to baggage claim, don't forget your damn gut on carousel six. You need that gut to steer you clearly and keep you on the path to making decisions that work in your favor.

Stay in your own lane. No matter how much you love or did love someone, how to fix their mistakes is none of your damn business. When you're so focused on another person, you neglect your bomb-ass life. You stop doing the things you enjoy. Let's be real; what fun is that? No matter if you're single, in a relationship, or going through a break-up, you need to do things that make you complete.

Stay present in the A and B because you have no control over your XYZ. Heads up—taking your obsessive mind away from someone else won't ruin the outcome you want for XYZ. It may just help you. It doesn't matter how much you obsess over the outcome; it will be what it will be.

When you show up for yourself and hit your basic needs, you no longer need to look for that in a partner. Sure, you might default to that at times when you're feeling lonely 'cause let's just face it, even superwoman has her setbacks every now and then.

No matter what your partner is doing or how they're showing up in a relationship, you're taking care of yourself. It would be extremely unrealistic to think that your partner can fill the needs that can only be met by you. Codependency tricks the mind into thinking you can fill their needs first. If only it worked that way, none of us would ever have to go through codependency.

To stay on the course of taking care of yourself, you need to know when to give yourself a little extra lovin'. Figuring out what's stopping you is the honey to the damn beehive. Whether it's a current or past relationship, looking at the fears causing all of this obsession can help you find your bearings.

Then, it's time to get intimate with yourself. What are the things that bring complete joy and purpose to your life? Often, my clients come to me and feel they don't have a true purpose. Usually, it boils down to living for someone else's purpose, hoping to make it their own. This goes back to banging your head against the wall, hoping the pain will subside.

Once you figure out your golden nugget of how you want to fill your life, go after it. There is no point in just daydreaming about what you want. That wouldn't be respectful to yourself. An action plan puts you in control of your own life. Fair warning, once you go after this, don't be surprised if you have an increase in happiness, self-esteem, and joy. That shit may become contagious. Just saying.

You can talk about making a change until your teeth fall out, but until you keep yourself accountable for making shit happen, nothing will happen. It's also easy to be inspired and take action and then find yourself falling short of continuing it, which sounds like zero fun. From someone who tried this loop a couple of times, it is zero fun.

Time is always on your side. By selecting a date to make a change, it helps you track your progress. Honesty creates momentum. You can create a space to let go of denial when you face what needs to be done.

Trust is there to help create a relationship with yourself. When committing to following through on something, you're creating trust within. By breaking this commitment, you'd be breaking trust with yourself.

Staying on track is the core ingredient to change. Remember, this isn't always going to be rainbows and butterflies. It may feel uncomfortable as hell, but once you follow through on your accountability, you'll be damn glad you did. I highly suggest you don't do it alone, either. Lean on your Hype Squad. Having a squad of people rooting for your success creates community. Within the community, you have belonging. You're not meant to go through hardships alone. At times in my life, I isolated myself. I learned the hard way, sister. That's not strength. That's ego.

Within the foundation of self-love, keep positive as you continue busting down the doors of codependency. There will be times when you take two steps forward and one step back. Keep in mind, you are moving forward one step at a time. The fact that you're here and you've made it this far is fucking amazing.

You're winning. Don't stop putting one foot in front of the other. Push through moments of doubt, and you will reach your potential of greatness. At times, it can feel impossible to get rid of the contagious love, but it's not. At the end of the day, it all starts with you. You've got to love your own damn self. And that shit—is contagious.

ABOUT THE AUTHOR

Author Carla Romo is a speaker and a certified dating and relationship coach. At age 24, she hit her rock bottom with yet another toxic codependent relationship. But, this time, she got up and learned how to break free from codependency for damn good. Inspired by her own self-growth journey, she took lemons and made lemonade. Today she is helping other women who feel stuck and stagnant build purpose in their dating life, break-ups, and relationships.

Aside from her coaching business, her passion lies in being an activist for women's rights. Carla served as a public official on the West Hollywood Women's Advisory Board working on California statewide and nationwide legislation. Before pivoting careers into the self-help coaching world, she cast and produced major TV network shows and produced a documentary called, "Luke & Jedi."

Today, Carla leads nationwide workshops and is a highly sought after motivational speaker on self-love and relationships. She has been featured on or collaborated with BRAVO, Cosmopolitan, Bumble, Lifetime, Bustle, The Knot, as well as high rated iTunes Podcasts.

Carla Romo is here to spread the message—the most important relationship you will ever have is with your damn self.

CONTACT ME

Hey girl!

Want to say hello?
Interested in coaching with me?
Want me to speak at your next event?

Email: carla@iamcarlaromo.com
Follow me on IG: @iamcarlaromo
Follow me on FB: @iamcarlaromo
www.iamcarlaromo.com

Made in the USA
Columbia, SC
21 September 2019